Opening up
Jonah

PAUL MACKRELL

DayOne

Opening up
Jonah

PAUL MACKRELL

'Jonah, a book full of surprises! God says, 'Go,' but Jonah says, 'No,' and runs away. He survives an unseasonable storm and a fish story that's hard to swallow, and all because of frightful Nineveh. Who would believe it? Well, thankfully, Paul Mackrell does, and in this fine work he not only sets the scene but shows the relevance for us today. It would be another surprise if many do not receive great benefit from this book.'

Clive Anderson
The Butts Church, Alton, Hampshire, England

'This kind of commentary on the Book of Jonah is long overdue and Paul Mackrell has filled that gap. He gives us clear and careful explanation of the text with very practical and useful suggestions for further study. His concise exposition of each chapter makes a very dramatic book all the more compelling to read. I believe that this commentary with its helpful insights will prove to be a great aid in personal devotions and for use in group Bible studies.'

William G Hughes
Pastor, Emmanuel Baptist Church, Coconut Creek, Florida, USA

© Day One Publications 2007
First printed 2007

Unless otherwise indicated, Scripture quotations in this publication are
from the Holy Bible: New International Version (NIV), copyright ©1973,
1978, 1984, International Bible Society.

ISBN 978-1-84625-080-4

9 781846 250804 >

British Library Cataloguing in Publication Data available

Published by Day One Publications
Ryelands Road, Leominster, HR6 8NZ
Telephone 01568 613 740 FAX 01568 611 473

email—sales@dayone.co.uk
web site—www.dayone.co.uk
North American—e-mail-sales@dayonebookstore.com
North American web site—www.dayonebookstore.com

All rights reserved
No part of this publication may be reproduced, or stored in a retrieval system, or
transmitted, in any form or by any means, mechanical, electronic, photocopying,
recording or otherwise, without the prior permission of Day One Publications.

Designed by Steve Devane and printed by Gutenberg Press, Malta

Dedication

This book is dedicated to Sue—the warmth of my life.

List of Bible abbreviations

THE OLD TESTAMENT		1 Chr.	1 Chronicles	Dan.	Daniel
		2 Chr.	2 Chronicles	Hosea	Hosea
Gen.	Genesis	Ezra	Ezra	Joel	Joel
Exod.	Exodus	Neh.	Nehemiah	Amos	Amos
Lev.	Leviticus	Esth.	Esther	Obad.	Obadiah
Num.	Numbers	Job	Job	Jonah	Jonah
Deut.	Deuteronomy	Ps.	Psalms	Micah	Micah
Josh.	Joshua	Prov.	Proverbs	Nahum	Nahum
Judg.	Judges	Eccles.	Ecclesiastes	Hab.	Habakkuk
Ruth	Ruth	S.of.S.	Song of Solomon	Zeph.	Zephaniah
1 Sam.	1 Samuel	Isa.	Isaiah	Hag.	Haggai
2 Sam.	2 Samuel	Jer.	Jeremiah	Zech.	Zechariah
1 Kings	1 Kings	Lam.	Lamentations	Mal.	Malachi
2 Kings	2 Kings	Ezek.	Ezekiel		

THE NEW TESTAMENT		Gal.	Galatians	Heb.	Hebrews
		Eph.	Ephesians	James	James
Matt.	Matthew	Phil.	Philippians	1 Peter	1 Peter
Mark	Mark	Col.	Colossians	2 Peter	2 Peter
Luke	Luke	1 Thes.	1 Thessalonians	1 John	1 John
John	John	2 Thes.	2 Thessalonians	2 John	2 John
Acts	Acts	1 Tim.	1 Timothy	3 John	3 John
Rom.	Romans	2 Tim.	2 Timothy	Jude	Jude
1 Cor.	1 Corinthians	Titus	Titus	Rev.	Revelation
2 Cor.	2 Corinthians	Philem.	Philemon		

Overview

Think Jonah, think whale. Or should we? Actually no. The whale, or great fish, merely appears among the list of supporting cast, along with the worm which appears in chapter 4.

Instead the book is about the character of God. It shows us something of his burning holiness, something of his powerful and detailed ordering of event and something of his tender mercy. None of this is stated as cold fact—the kind of thing you might find in a text-book on theology. Rather these truths about the Lord emerge as the plot unravels. His character shines through as conversations and events are played out before our eyes.

The pagan city of Nineveh had to be warned that their evil was so offensive to the Lord that he had fixed a day of judgement. It was to fall after forty days. Yet the very fact that a date had been set in the calendar held out a hope, however slight it may have seemed, that judgement could be averted. Would they take this message seriously? If so, what would they do or say during those 40 days to dissuade God from the course of action he had promised to take?

Jonah, God's chosen envoy to Nineveh, had to learn that God's purposes could not be thwarted. His attempted

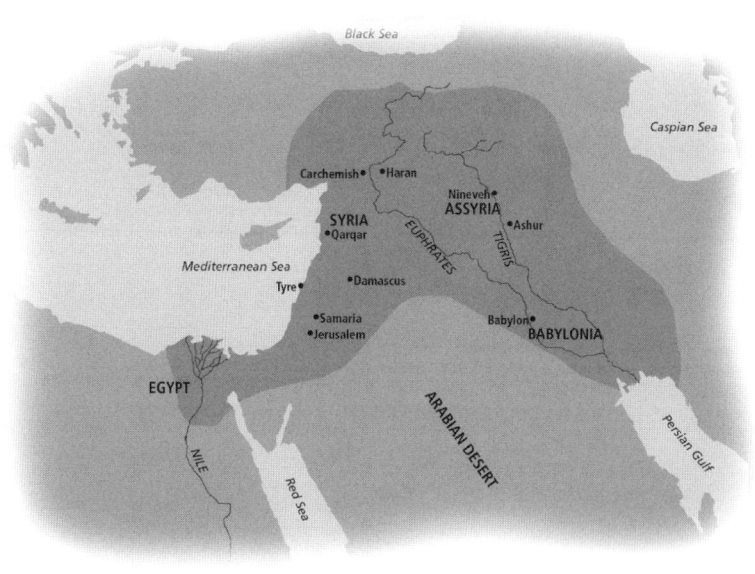

KINGS OF JUDAH	JEROBOAM II (782 TO 753)	VARIOUS KINGS	PEKAH (740–731)
KINGS OF ASSYRIA	*ASHUR-DAN III* *(772 TO 754)*	*ASHUR-NIRARI V* *(754 TO 744)*	*ASHUR-NIRARI V* *(754 TO 744)*

780 **770** **760** **750** **740** **730**   **612**

JONAH GOES TO NINEVEH	THE DEPORTATION OF ISRAEL STARTS 733	FALL OF NINEVEH (612)

resignation was not accepted by the Lord. Nineveh had to hear God's word, and they had to hear it from the lips of Jonah.

Finally, both Jonah, and the people he represented, had to learn that God's mercy is neither handed out nor withheld according to a scale measuring how deserving or undeserving an individual or a nation might be. God's mercy reached Jonah in the depths of the sea. It also reached Nineveh in the depths of its wickedness. Neither one was deserving.

Jonah is fond of the word 'great'. In the book we meet a great fish, a great storm and a great city. But, above all, we are introduced to a great God.

We can summarize the book as follows:

Chapter 1—Jonah running from God; God chasing him down.

Chapter 2—Jonah praying to the Lord his God from 'the depths'.

Chapter 3—Jonah preaching in Nineveh; widespread repentance.

Chapter 4—Jonah sulking in self-pitying depression; God teaching him.

The book is often treated as an allegory or myth, but there is little reason to treat it any differently from the way in which the book itself is presented to us—as sober history. Certainly that is how the Lord himself took it (Matt. 12:40).

Background and Summary

The northern Iraqi city of Mosul sits on the western bank of the River Tigris. Across the river on the opposite bank lie two mounds. These mounds mark ancient Nineveh, much of which is buried beneath them. Nineveh was once a glorious city, the capital of Assyria and centre of a proud and militaristic empire. But now all that remains are these ruins.

The Bible has a surprising amount to tell us about Nineveh. It records its beginnings. In Genesis 10:11 we learn that its founding father was Nimrod. And we are there at the end, too. In the book of Nahum we read the sombre description of Nineveh's fall in 612 BC, prophesied ahead of time. Speaking through Nahum, the Lord leaves no one in any doubt as to why his hand of judgement would shortly fall.

Sandwiched between the beginning and the end of Nineveh's eventful life is what should be seen as her finest hour. Unexpectedly, it was not the scene of a great military triumph, though she could boast many such conquests. Rather it was when she renounced her cruel and violent ways. And at the preaching of Jonah, highly reluctant and disobedient though he was, the people of Nineveh turned to the Lord en masse. Their repentance may not have lasted for more than a generation, but for the time being it was deep and sincere. It also extended throughout all levels of society.

As Jonah walked through that impressive and frightening city 2,800 years ago, nothing could have seemed more unlikely than her sudden ruin. Nineveh provided the last word in military strength and security. Her walls were one hundred feet in height and built on a rock foundation. Overshadowing the walls were 1,500 watchtowers, some two hundred feet in height. Everything about this mighty city said that she would last for centuries.

> This cannot be explained other than through the powerful working of a sovereign God who can direct the hearts of men as easily as he can control the appetite of a great fish or a tiny worm.

A bedraggled and lonely foreigner walking city streets and shouting a repeated message would normally be ridiculed without mercy. Even more strange was the message itself— 'Forty more days and Nineveh will be overthrown.' Two remarkable facts strike us with considerable force here: first, that Nineveh could possibly be overthrown within forty days, and second, that anyone should believe such a message.

Yet believe him they did. This cannot be explained other than through the powerful working of a sovereign God who can direct the hearts of men as easily as he can control the appetite of a great fish or a tiny worm. In considerable distress and sorrow they turned from their wickedness and pleaded the mercy of God. Given the character of God revealed in the Bible, the result was inevitable—'when God saw what they did and how they turned from their evil ways, he had compassion and did not bring upon them the destruction he had threatened.' (Jonah 3:10)

Amazingly, Jonah's unbelievable success was met by a deep despondency and resentment on his part. Nineveh's salvation was something he dreaded. He had prophesied her demise with relish—with all his soul he wanted it to happen. He observed her repentance with dismay. Apart from anything else, it meant that he would go down in the annals of Nineveh as a false prophet—the man who had foretold their ruin and been proved embarrassingly wrong.

Ironically, had the Ninevites disbelieved and disregarded Jonah, judgement would have swept them away. Jonah would have watched with smug delight and thought to himself, 'Well, I told them so.' He considered that of all the places on earth, Nineveh deserved the judgement he had been sent to proclaim.

It is now that we perceive Jonah's unwillingness to obey God's express command to go to Nineveh in the first place and proclaim the message he would give him. That unwillingness hardened into outright disobedience and a futile attempt to run from the Lord. Chapter 1 is a sea-chase. Despite a head start, the prospect of escaping the God who cares both for the soul of Jonah as well as for the souls of the Ninevites was hopelessly doomed. The Lord caught him. Even then Jonah's stubbornness was absolute. In desperation he opts for the ultimate way out of his ridiculous, self-imposed dilemma. Drowning seems preferable to obeying the living God.

Chapter 2 sees Jonah coming to his senses. After being thrown overboard he sinks below the waves. It is brinkmanship of the highest order but as the final seconds of his life ebb away he cries out in desperation to the Lord. From the depths he is heard, and the great fish fulfils its God-appointed commission and swallows Jonah. Such a sudden and dramatic answer to prayer gives Jonah hope that he will come through this experience and live to serve God again. This time deliverance is slow in coming. He remains in the belly of the great fish for three days.

> Jonah has demonstrated great determination in the most foolish of ventures—that of running from the presence of the Lord. Now the Lord will demonstrate an even greater determination.

Jonah has demonstrated great determination in the most foolish of ventures—that of running from the presence of the Lord. Now the Lord will demonstrate an even greater determination, but this time in an altogether more noble cause. He will have Nineveh hear the message he wants them to hear. What is more, they will hear it by the mouth of Jonah. This reluctant prophet is given another chance to serve his Lord. The fish vomits Jonah on the dry land and the mission to Nineveh is back on.

Following the repentance of the people and the forgiveness

of the Lord in chapter 3, the book closes with Jonah being taught a profound lesson—the value of a soul. The Lord takes his tantrum-throwing child and patiently instructs him. Through some harsh practical lessons, Jonah is shown something of the heart of God and made to see the sheer breadth of his grace to the undeserving. And sitting astride the heap of the undeserving is not the wicked king of Nineveh, but Jonah himself.

Did Jonah learn his lesson? Most probably. Otherwise, it seems unlikely that the book could ever have been written. Sadly Nineveh itself forgot the lesson it had heard in such dramatic style. Less than 200 years later another judgement was pronounced against her. This time there was no repentance and no reprieve. Nineveh fell to the Babylonians.

Those two remaining mounds stand as a stark warning. One of them is known as 'Nebu Yunas' (mound of Jonah). Some Muslims claim that this is where Jonah's body lies buried. As unlikely as that may seem, it is not altogether impossible. In any event it suggests that Jonah had been greatly honoured among the Ninevites. They rightly acknowledged him as the prophet who served to avert what would later befall them. The other mound ought to stand for the prophet Nahum—the faithful prophet who spoke God's word and was not heeded.

Both books—Jonah and Nahum—stand today as the living testimony of God. We can read them and say, 'He told us so.'

For further study ▶

FOR FURTHER STUDY

1. What could be the significance in the number of days God gave Nineveh? See Genesis 7:4, 17 and Matthew 4:1-2 for other instances of forty days. Numbers 14:33 refers to forty years.

2. What do Jonah 1:17; 4:6 and 4:7 tell us about God's control?

TO THINK ABOUT AND DISCUSS

1. What does Jonah's commission to go to Nineveh tell us about God's concern for other nations, even in the Old Testament? (See Acts 11:18.)

2. What is the difference between a false prophet and a failing prophet? Jonah's prophecy about Nineveh did not come to pass. Did that make him a false prophet?

3. Nineveh eventually fell and was plundered as prophesied in Nahum 2:6-10 and 3:7. What does this say about each generation needing to respond to God's call to repent and turn to him?

1 Oh, for the wings of a dove

(1:1-3)

Few of the Old Testament prophets saw any fruit for their labours. Mostly they were ridiculed or ignored altogether, but still they kept going. Jonah was an exception in two ways. First, he was spectacularly successful, both at home and abroad. Second, he deeply resented the task God had appointed him and, for that reason, he ran away.

Jonah the 'Homing-Bird'

Jonah means 'dove'. We usually think of a dove as a symbol of peace. Bearing in mind how desperate Jonah was to watch Nineveh receive the devastating punishment he felt she so richly deserved (4:5), he seems more of a hawk than a dove. But a dove is also a home-loving bird, and in that respect Jonah was well suited to his name. More than anything he loved his own nation and people. The trouble was that it excluded everyone else. This fierce and narrow nationalism is the key to his stubborn disobedience. It is also the character trait that God addresses throughout the book.

The home mission

The book of Jonah is concerned entirely with Jonah's mission to Nineveh, the great city of Assyria—the 'away mission'. His mission at home, on the other hand, is recounted in a few verses (2 Kings 14:23-27). It fixes Jonah in history, ministering during the long and successful reign of Jeroboam II, king of Israel. The striking feature of his task is the fact that he brings a positive message from the Lord at a time of national idolatry and immorality. Jeroboam II, like the many kings before him, led his people into sin and consequent misery. Yet the Lord sees their suffering and, with no one else to help them, steps in to give relief. Jonah is directed to prophesy that the country's borders, which had been eaten away through repeated foreign incursions, would be restored. That is indeed what happened. No doubt Jonah's popularity rose as he prophesied and soared off the graph as the prophecy was fulfilled.

The lesson to be learned from this particular incident is that the Lord pities the undeserving. It is a lesson which is repeated throughout Jonah's life. It had to be, since he was such a slow learner. He will learn it on a personal level (chapter 2). He will also learn it in relation to the wicked Ninevites (chapters 3 and 4).

Nineveh the Great (v. 2)

Nineveh was great in size, great in power and great in military prowess. There were around five times as many people living there as lived in Jerusalem. A more impressive city could not be found. From God's perspective she was also great in wickedness. It was this which literally came up before his face. The God who sees all, hears all and understands all, also smells all. And Nineveh stank.

The reaction of the Lord to such wickedness was unwavering. He was *against* it. Many will come to the book of Jonah and have a fairly good idea as to how things will turn out. They know beforehand that Nineveh will repent of her wickedness and that the Lord will turn from the judgement he had promised. This is set out for us in chapter 3. But we should not let prior knowledge deflect us from grasping verse 2 in its stark awfulness. In reality Nineveh was against the Lord, whether she realized it or not. That in itself was dangerous enough. But their situation was actually far worse—the Lord was against *them*. Notice that it is not a case of 'hating the sin but loving the sinner'. The Lord is certainly against the wickedness of Nineveh, but he is also against Nineveh herself—the perpetrator of the sin.

Nonetheless, even in these bleak words, there is a strong ray of hope. Forty is often the period of testing (the number of years the Israelites spent in the wilderness, the number of days the Lord Jesus Christ was tested, and so on). Here was a period of testing for the Ninevites—would they heed what God said through Jonah and turn from their wicked ways?

As well as that, Jonah's task was not just foretelling the future. If the destruction of Nineveh had been written in concrete without any chance of being revoked, what was the point of sending someone to tell them? If there was nothing the people of Nineveh could do to avoid the predicted disaster, telling them would be mockery rather than a warning. Also, what would it say of the character of God? As it was, Jonah knew God better than that (4:2).

The Word of the Lord (v. 1)

The book opens with the Lord directing Jonah to get up. Nineveh is over 600 miles away, but its inhabitants must hear what God wants to say to them. The Lord could use means other than people, but he chooses not to do so. He could also use methods other than preaching, but again he chooses not to do so. So Jonah is directed to go and preach against the city. He is hardly what you would call an outstanding example as a prophet. Surely there were better men God could have raised up and used? Indeed, yes. But the Lord is determined not only that Nineveh is to hear his word through human lips, but also through the lips of a flawed and failing believer like Jonah. The Lord has his own plans for this important mission, and personnel are at the heart of it.

It seems so obvious but Jonah cannot stand on his own doorstep and decry the violence and immorality of people who are not there. He must stand face to face with Ninevites, meet their eyes, and faithfully relate God's word. He must go to them.

God's word to Jonah is to 'get up and go'. Is there an implied criticism here? Is he idling away his time when he should be on his feet already? Certainly the ship's captain later on had cause to think so (v. 6). In any event the Lord is calling him to immediate service. Jonah is to go to Nineveh and he is to go *now*.

Running from the Lord

Having been told to get up, Jonah gets up. But instead of going north and east, he chooses west. To use a British analogy, directed to the John O'Groats of his known world, he opts for Land's End instead. He does not argue with God about the mission; he simply runs from it. It is an in-your-face act of disobedience. Why? It was not because he was frightened, even though he had good reason to be. Neither did he fear ridicule, although a lone figure shouting out that Nineveh, with its massive walls and military might, was about to be overthrown would certainly invite it.

> Jonah does not argue with God about the mission; he simply runs from it. It is an in-your-face act of disobedience.

No, Jonah's problem was the message itself. God told him to say, 'Forty more days and Nineveh will be overturned' (3:4). He was perfectly comfortable with prophesying judgement and destruction. In fact he warmed to it. But he choked on the forty days. It meant that there was just a possibility that God could be persuaded to relent. As we will see his fears would be realized.

So he buys his one-way ticket and runs from the Lord—or at least tries to. You would have thought Jonah ought to have known that nobody can ever escape from God. Indeed he did know it. Not only would he have been familiar with Psalm 139, but telling the sailors about fearing the Lord, the God of heaven who has made the sea and the dry land in verse 9 shows that at one level he believed it. But sin warps the thinking. What he knew in his head was distorted by a mind set on disobedience. He was also running from before the face of the Lord—the place of service. It was a case of resigning his calling.

The folly of running

Jonah was running from the presence of God. This was madness. Jonah knew the Psalms and knew what David was talking about when he spoke of being filled 'with joy' in the presence of the Lord and of 'eternal pleasures at your right hand' (Ps. 16:11). That thought ought to have troubled him. What was he doing fleeing the place where fulfilment and joy met? So determined was he upon this course of action that he would take it, even if it led to death. Ultimately he opts for suicide before repentance.

But as Jonah makes his way to the quayside at Joppa, there was probably very little hint of what was to come. The day may have dawned bright and sunny. Everything seems to work out well: a ship is there; it happens to be going just where Jonah is

> Of greater significance is the Tarshish of Jonah's dreams—the place where he sought peace and fulfilment away from the presence and service of the Lord. In God's grace he failed to arrive. The reality is that Tarshish does not exist; it is only the place of disobedient dreams.

headed and Jonah has the right money. There is even a possibility that he may have financed the entire voyage. The thought of leaving family and friends was perhaps submerged beneath the exciting prospects of a new life beckoning. You could even imagine him finding some ironic amusement in singing the words of Psalm 55:6: 'Oh, that I had the wings of a dove! [literally, the wings of a Jonah] I would fly away and be at rest.'

As the ship left port, conditions for Jonah, both within and without, were set to change.

Tarshish

And so Jonah sails for Tarshish. Commentators speculate about where Tarshish might be and usually suggest a destination in southern Spain. Since he never got there it hardly matters now.

Of greater significance is the Tarshish of Jonah's dreams—the place where he sought peace and fulfilment away from the presence and service of the Lord. In God's grace he failed to arrive. The reality is that Tarshish does not exist; it is only the place of disobedient dreams.

For further study ▶

FOR FURTHER STUDY

1. Read Genesis 11:1-9 where the people proudly attempt to build a city and a tower that reaches to the heavens. It is a forerunner of many great cities, including Nineveh and Babylon, which typify humanity organized in opposition to God. The tower is left in ruins, but consider what does come up before the Lord (v. 2).

2. Read Acts 10. Reflect on the place of Joppa as a cross-roads in the experience of both Jonah and Peter. It was here that both men were confronted with the question as to whom the gospel is for.

TO THINK ABOUT AND DISCUSS

1. It is tempting to think that circumstances fitting together well proves that a course of action must be the will of God. Why would Jonah have been wrong to have reached such a conclusion when everything worked together to help him run away?

2. How does the death of Jesus Christ turn the Father from being the one who is against us, because of our sin, into the one of whom the apostle Paul spoke when he asked: 'If God is for us, who can be against us?' (Rom. 8:31)

3. Are there situations from which we wish to run? Are we harbouring dreams of our own little Tarshish—a place where we disengage from the Christian battle or the place of service? Do we imagine it to be a place of peace and rest? If so, what does the message of Jonah have to say?

2 Those in peril on the sea

(1: 4-6)

The original language repeatedly records Jonah as going 'down'. In 1:3 he goes down to Joppa and then down to the ship. In 1:5 he goes down into the hold and, finally, in 2:6 he sinks down into death itself. Not so much a record of his geographical location, this is a chart of his moral decline. What may have begun as a small hesitant step as he set off for Joppa has quickened into a purposeful stride. Before long he is fleeing 'from the LORD' (v. 3).

The footsteps of God

What Jonah did not realize was that he was being chased. God was after him. At first God's voice in his conscience may have been like a gentle tap on the shoulder. But as Jonah hardens in his resolve to block out the voice of the Lord, that voice becomes ever louder. In the full teeth of the storm the gentle shoulder tap will become a violent shaking of his wayward prophet.

Jonah continues to shut his ears to God. He comforts himself with the thought that he must defend the justice and holiness of God, even if God himself will not do it. He tells himself that no self-respecting prophet, asked to hold out a message of hope to Israel's pagan enemy, could possibly contemplate doing anything other than what he is now doing—running away. But all this has worn him out. He lays down his deadened senses and flattened conscience, falling asleep in a state of backslidden stupor and self-justifying arguments (v. 5). Meanwhile God's footsteps are closing in.

The storm

We know from the New Testament that Jesus can calm the storm. We rightly take comfort in learning that his power is unchanged, and that the focus of his care in working all things together for the good of those who love him is still the same. But we should also understand that the God who stills the storm, also sends it (v. 4).

This was no ordinary storm. These sailors would have braved out many Mediterranean squalls in the past, including perhaps some winter storms on the odd occasion when they dared to put to sea outside the safe sailing season between the end of April and the middle of September. But this was a category of storm none of them had faced before. It was 'a great wind'. Its ferocity instilled an intense fear among the entire crew, without exception (v. 5). What is more, there was no let-up in the storm. Having hit the ship with extreme and sudden force, the storm intensified and the sea grew rougher than ever (vv. 11, 13).

The Lord does not merely send storms—quite literally, he hurls them. The same Hebrew word occurs three times in chapter 1. In verse 4 he hurls the storm; in verse 5 the sailors hurl the cargo into the sea, and in verse 15 they hurl Jonah overboard. The hurling is not the action of a frustrated deity petulantly throwing a tantrum and taking revenge on the man who refused to do his bidding. Rather, it indicates precision and purpose in God's actions. He is not out to punish Jonah, but to turn him round and restore him. .

Lessons from storms

In life we all face storms from time to time. Sometimes they take us completely by surprise. Often they are severe and without respite. From an emotional and psychological point of view, they can be explosive and violent. But the great design of the divine storm-thrower is an entirely benevolent and gracious one. His purpose is that those who belong to him through faith in Christ should learn to trust him more through the storms. The aim is that the believer will become more like the Lord Jesus Christ—a process called 'sanctification'.

There is nothing mechanical about this process. Merely being confronted with a storm does not mean the individual believer will automatically emerge from the trial in a healthier spiritual condition. Tragically, storms leave some people in a bitter state of self-pity. A trail of devastation can be scarred on some people's hearts for the rest of their earthly days. Others, however, face the wildest of storms and emerge triumphant and stronger, testifying to the Lord's keeping power.

Responses to the storm

Everything depends on how the storm is faced. Here we see a number of different reactions.

THE REACTION OF RESIGNED DESPAIR

It is strange to think of an inanimate object like a ship having a response, but the literal reading is that the ship 'thought to break up'. If the ship imagined she was going to pieces, she was right—she was. With the planks creaking at the force of the pounding waves and with water seeping through the opening timbers, her plight was indeed desperate. The reaction of some people to the storms they face is much the same. They groan with self-pity and imagine they must be falling apart. Like a rudderless ship being tossed to and fro, they are completely at the mercy of the storm. But what may be justified in an unthinking ship is pitiful in a human being. We are not pathetic corks without direction or purpose. We are thinking beings with a degree of control over our reactions and emotions. We know how we ought to behave in the storm and what we should believe through it. It may not be easy, but when the storm arrives we can, at the very least, begin by reminding ourselves who sent it. And then we can ask what we can learn from it and through it.

THE REACTION OF FEAR

The sailors were petrified (v. 5). They thought they were going to die. Like so many in our own culture, they had no hope of anything beyond the grave. Their faith in their gods was sincere enough, but each one was unable to offer any assurance as to what might await any individual follower when life ended. In short, they were no-gods. Unable to answer prayer in life, what hope was there for the final prayer in death? And so for the sailors it was ultimately the fear of the unknown, and for them nothing was more unknown than death itself.

THE REACTION OF ORGANIZED RELIGION

In verse 5 each of the sailors cried out to his own god. It was a kind of disorganized and panic-stricken ecumenical service on deck. The sailors were aware that this storm had a divine origin but were struggling to find out which particular deity they ought to be addressing. In plying its trade across the Mediterranean Sea, the ship would routinely lose the odd crew member as she called into port, and a replacement would have to be recruited. This would give a cosmopolitan mix to the ship's company, which found expression in the many different deities represented. With such an impressive array of idols on display, there was a good chance that the one responsible for the storm would own up and respond to their heartfelt cries. It was important that everyone on board played his part and prayed to the deity to which he owed allegiance. Between them they ought to hit on the right one. But what good is all this organization unless someone engages with the Lord who had sent the storm in the first place? And there was no one.

THE REACTION OF SECULAR COMMON SENSE

Some people display admirable leadership skills in a crisis. The captain seems to have been just such an example, organizing the men into hurling the cargo overboard—a move designed to help the lightened ship ride over the waves, rather than sinking down into them. The trouble is that it does not work. This storm has been divinely commissioned, and an approach which only addresses the symptoms rather than the cause is doomed to fail. Without grappling with the divine dimension of the problem they faced, a permanent solution would for ever elude them.

THE REACTION OF ESCAPISM

Running away had become a habit with Jonah. Having run from the Lord, he runs from the confusion and turmoil going on all around him and finds a hiding place. Unlike the Lord Jesus who fell asleep in a boat amidst a storm after a weary day's work, Jonah's sleep is that of the idle, guilt-ridden escapist. The methods people use to try and blot out life's problems are many and varied. Virtually anything that can distract will suffice, at least for the time being. And that is precisely the problem—'for the time being' always runs out with at ultimate day of reckoning at the end of it. Sleeping his troubles away would provide a temporary respite for Jonah, but reality is never far away and Jonah is roused by a captain shocked at finding him. He scornfully asks, 'How can you sleep?' He might have said: 'What on earth do you think you're playing at?' It is the

> Unlike the Lord Jesus who fell asleep in a boat amidst a storm after a weary day's work, Jonah's sleep is that of the idle, guilt-ridden escapist.

one question Jonah manages to sidestep throughout this opening chapter.

THE MISSING REACTION

Having listed negative examples of how not to react in a crisis, we ought to be concluding with a positive example of how it should have been done. But there was no such example. It should have come from Jonah, but his was the worst reaction of all. He alone had someone to pray to and who would listen, but from Jonah there was only silence. Where we should have been reading about courageous faith in action, there was mere selfish withdrawal.

The grace of God

Lots of prayers had gone up and much fervour had been expended. But all of it had been in the direction of stone-deaf, lifeless, impotent idols. The total lack of response was utterly predictable and inevitable. Only Jonah had a route into the presence of the living God who had sent the storm and who alone could still it, but he was not on speaking terms with him. The question is therefore: will God step in when nobody has sought his help?

The answer is 'yes'. Jonah has failed the sailors miserably, but the Lord will not. What a low view we have of him if we think he will only be stirred into action if we hit on the right formula in our approach to him. It is surely man-centred and even superstitious to believe he will only hear us once we have clocked up the required number of hours in prayer, or that unless we get a decent-sized number of people joining together he is really not that bothered. This is a wrong idea of prayer. Answers to prayer do not depend upon weight of numbers or length of time at the praying end, but on the character and purposes of the one at the answering end.

The captain

The captain told Jonah to call on his god because 'maybe he will take notice of us, and we will not perish'. If he was right in his suspicion that Jonah was the key to unravelling the mystery of the storm, the trail must lead back to the God Jonah claimed to serve. Perhaps it was only a final straw, but they were drowning and the captain would clutch it anyway. If Jonah could but call on his god, maybe Jonah's god could, just possibly, spare a thought and save them.

Jonah may have burbled out a promise to the captain that, of course, he would pray. But how could he? Speaking to the Lord was utterly out of the question for a stubbornly unrepentant Jonah. The captain wanted him to say or do something to placate the wrath of the deity who had sent the storm, but Jonah said and did nothing,

It is now that we see the grace of God in all its sublime beauty. The Lord takes the initiative and steps in with strength and purpose. He will certainly spare them a thought, and these men will not perish.

Let us take this a stage further. Man can do nothing to placate the wrath of God against sin, but God takes the initiative and steps in with grace and power. He spares far more than a passing thought; he gives up his one and only Son who bears the wrath of God in his own body on the cross as he bears our sin. In Romans 8:32 we read that God 'did not spare his own Son, but gave him up for us all.'

The captain was concerned lest he and his men should perish. He was thinking of the immediate. God's actions indicate that the immediate was not unimportant to him either, but there is an eternal perishing which should be of surpassing concern to us. How comforting then the words of the Lord Jesus Christ: 'For God so loved the world that he gave his one and only Son, that whoever believes in him shall not perish but have eternaal life' (John 3:16).

For further study ▶

FOR FURTHER STUDY

1. Read Acts 27. How do Paul's faith and actions compare with what you find in Jonah?
2. Read Romans 13:11-14, Ephesians 5:8-14 and 1 Thessalonians 5:4-8. While recognizing the proper place for sleep and rest, Christians are called to be awake. Why was Jonah's sleep so offensive to the captain, and what are the characteristics of sleep which are to be avoided?

TO THINK ABOUT AND DISCUSS

1. When storms come our way, how can we look at them from a divine perspective? What should we ask from God in them?
2. The ship with its pagan sailors can be compared to the world as it struggles for survival with its conflicting ideas. What does this say to us if we consider Jonah to be a picture of a sleeping church?
3. The false god Baal was worshipped by the Hittites and many others nations around the Mediterranean basin and beyond. He was the god of storm, often depicted with a thunder club in his right hand and a lightning fork in the left. How does that image differ from the reality of the God who was behind this storm?

3 Mind the gap

(1:7-10)

Some underground and railway platforms in Britain are curved. Any passenger getting on or off needs to be careful since there may be a gap in between the platform and the train itself. It is therefore common to hear a taped recording being repeated over the tannoy as each successive train pulls up—'Mind the gap, mind the gap!'

Jonah's search for a quiet and peaceful life outside the purposes of God was proving to be more elusive than ever. It may have appeared within reach as he stood on the dockside at Joppa, but all that had vanished amidst the turmoil of the storm and the very real prospect of the ship sinking.

Now, to add to his woes, he faces a barrage of questions from the sailors, part accusing and part inquisitive. He seeks to answer them honestly, but it exposes a massive gap between what he professes with his mouth and what he actually does in practice. It is an important lesson for us all. God says to us, 'Mind the gap.'

The lots (v. 7)

By now the sailors are in a state of desperation. They are fighting a losing battle in keeping the ship together and keeping the water out. They need to get to the bottom of what this storm is all about, and so they break off from their duties of bailing out and lightening the ship in order to throw lots. The lots only show what we, as readers, know all along—Jonah is the culprit. He is the cause of the trouble, calamity or evil, as the word may be translated.

There are several instances in the Bible where lots are thrown. It may seem to be an entirely arbitrary method of determining a question, but Proverbs 16:33 says: 'The lot is cast into the lap, but its every decision is from the LORD.' By now the finger is pointing very firmly at Jonah, but the sailors are still not absolutely convinced. They need to question him in order to make sure.

Questions Jonah cannot ignore (v. 8)

The first question amounts to a call to Jonah to come clean. Will he own up and admit that he is the source of trouble on this voyage? But before he can answer, more questions come tumbling out, fired at him from all quarters. The sailors want to find out what Jonah could possibly have done to merit such divine attention. Maybe Jonah himself did not know and the case needed some detective work to discover what prompted such anger. So could Jonah please retrace his steps? Was it something he had done, or some shady business he was about? Or somewhere he had been? Or the place and people he belonged to?

Perhaps at this point Jonah begins to have doubts about how solid his position really was. Until now he has been perfectly comfortable with running away, believing it was only what any reasonable, self-respecting Israelite would have done in the same situation. As far as he was concerned, it was utterly impossible to comply with God's wish to assign him to Nineveh. He felt it was morally repugnant to hold out the prospect of mercy to wicked pagans like the Ninevites. As far as Jonah was concerned, the problem was with God, not him.

But there are little clues that the Lord is now beginning to close in on Jonah and will not let him rest in his self-justifying arrogance. The words of the captain in verse 6 to 'get up and call on your god' would surely remind him of what God had said to him in verse 1—to get up and preach. Now the finger of God is pointing at Jonah, even in the chance throw of the lots. Everything is saying to him, 'Think again, Jonah.'

Jonah's reply (v. 9)

At face value Jonah's answer is exemplary: 'I am a Hebrew and I worship the LORD, the God of heaven, who made the sea and the land.' You could hardly wish for a more clear-cut statement of faith. There is nothing vague about it—he does not seek to side-step embarrassing questions with a half-hearted mumble about going to church. He speaks of his God and identifies him as Jehovah or Yahweh, the God who can be known and worshipped personally, as he himself does. What is more, his testimony is up to date. He does not reluctantly admit to a past adherence to this religion, partly through upbringing and partly through the immaturity of youth. Rather, he owns this God and confesses to a living, present-tense faith.

Until now the sailors have been desperately searching among an array of territorial gods for the one with whom they should be dealing. Each idol possessed its own adherents who claimed that their god ruled certain areas of land or water. The test was finding the one who controlled the grid lines within which they were battling for their lives. Jonah tells them they need look no further—Jehovah made it all. He made both the sea (where they were) and the land (where they wanted to be).

> How can an admiring but guilt-ridden bystander know that God's mercy is available for him too through faith alone in Jesus Christ, unless someone tells him?

There is even a challenge to these seamen. Implicitly, if there is a God who rules the sea and the land, any faith which pays homage to a lesser god claiming to govern just a portion of it can be safely discarded. Bearing in mind the proven impotence of any of these gods to answer a single prayer offered up with such desperate and heartfelt cries, the case for jettisoning their idols and turning to the Lord was compelling.

The case for clear testimonies

The world needs to hear testimonies like the one Jonah gave. Creation has a voice; it speaks of God, but cannot tell you how to find him. A godly life also has a voice. It may say that there is clear evidence of the influence of divine grace in that individual life, but that's all. How can an admiring but guilt-ridden bystander know that God's mercy is available for him too through faith alone in Jesus Christ, unless someone tells him? The life of the Son of God was uniquely perfect. Those around him could have learnt so much from simply watching and observing, and some of them did. However, the Father spoke from heaven and told them to 'listen to him' (Matt. 17:5). He came as the living Word of God. First and foremost we are to *hear* him. Having then heard, the church's task is to go into all the world and *preach* the gospel (Mark 16:15).

The sailors' reaction (v. 10)

Already in fear for their lives, the sailors were terror-stricken. You can almost see their mouths fall open as they exclaim with one voice: 'What have you done?' It was not a question that sought an answer, but a subdued expression of amazement and horror. Jonah's admission that he was running away had almost certainly come out in answering their questions, rather than something he had volunteered earlier in the voyage. It is not the mere fact that he is on the run that shocks them, but that he is on the run from such a God as this. How could he be so reckless and foolhardy? They stare aghast at Jonah. They at least have grasped the appalling seriousness of the situation, even if it still seems to have escaped Jonah.

The credibility gap

It was here that the chasm between what Jonah professed

with his lips and the life that he was living gaped the widest. The sailors have had their world turned upside down—almost literally. With Jonah's explanation in verse 9, a new understanding of the world is beginning to take shape in their minds, although their chances of remaining in it for much longer seem to be fast disappearing. Even so, they cannot fathom how Jonah can have behaved in such a way when he confesses knowing and worshipping the God who controls everything.

The words seemed to trip off Jonah's tongue so easily, but what about his life? As important as the verbal testimony is, we have to ask about the supporting evidence. The point is that the Christian is not just called to give evidence—he must *be* evidence. This is not merely saying that it is really helpful if he or she can produce something visible to back up the words; it is saying that the life and everything else that goes with it will inevitably and unavoidably be evidence itself. So the only question is this—is the testimony supported or contradicted? And, since there will always be some margin of human frailty and shortcomings, just how wide is the gap?

Lessons

There are vital lessons here for all who profess to worship and serve the same God Jonah alleged to serve. So we ask: since this is a God of holiness, where is the purity of life in speech, thought, deed, motive? He is also a God of power; so where is our faith day by day? He too is a God of compassion and love. This entitles us to ask about Jonah's compassion for the pagan sailors, but it also entitles others to ask about ours. Since the God we serve is a God of truth, should not his ambassadors be open and honest in their dealings with people? And finally, since he is the God of life, why do we seek life in the broken cisterns of this world rather than at his hand? We may criticize Jonah for dreaming that Tarshish could ever be what his soul longed for, but what of our own dreams of success, fulfilment and acceptance in this life?

God's purposes

As Jonah stands humiliated by accusing questions which expose the yawning credibility gap in his life, we should not forget that the Lord's purposes do not stop at embarrassing Jonah in front of the ungodly. He aims to restore Jonah, not punish him. Jonah's rightful place is in useful, God-honouring service. Even if there will be times of hardship and troubles, the Lord has something better for Jonah than the misery of his self-inflicted disobedience.

For further study ▶

FOR FURTHER STUDY

1. Read Jeremiah 10:1-10 and compare the worthless wooden idols with the true and living God.

2. Read Acts 10. Cornelius seemed such an exemplary and upright character that at first sight it is difficult to see what he could possibly need. Yet consider the extraordinary lengths that the Holy Spirit goes to in order to bring Peter and Cornelius into contact with each other. What does this say about the importance of Peter's words, and the inadequacy of Cornelius' very upright and religious life?

TO THINK ABOUT AND DISCUSS

1. In today's western society it is considered a good thing to have a private faith so long as it is kept under wraps. It is looked upon with suspicion if it ventures out into the world all around us. What does this passage say about such an approach?

2. Jonah seems to have embodied the spirit of the nation of Israel that he so loved. She, too, boasted an impressive outward profession, but a life which flatly contradicted it. Israel's ultimate destiny was to be taken away into captivity by the Assyrians whose capital was Nineveh. What does this say about God's long-term view of such a credibility gap?

3. The gods of the sailors were wooden, man-made objects. But their actions held together in the light of their beliefs (they knew that they were dependent on something or someone greater than themselves). Consider the sub-plot of chapter 1 and chart the initial attachment of the sailors to their idols, their sincerity of belief and practice, their disappointment in them and readiness to be open to other views, and their ultimately successful search for the living God.

4 Serendipity:discovering the unexpected

(1:11-17)

All of us at some time or another have stumbled across something we had previously lost or forgotten. It may be that this 'find' turns up in the course of looking for something else we had mislaid. The pleasant surprise of discovering the unexpected is called serendipity.

Perhaps this is not quite what happened to the pagan sailors in these verses, but in their search for a god to deliver them from the crisis they faced, they came across the God of heaven and earth. The discovery came as a total surprise to them, and if 'pleasant' is not the word they would have used, he was far more wonderful than they could have imagined. In short, they sought a deity to be pacified, but discovered a sovereign with a gracious purpose to all he does.

Seeking advice (vv. 11, 12)

With the ship breaking up amidst a worsening storm, the

situation has deteriorated alarmingly. The sailors know that they are now in a life-and-death struggle. They had realized early on that the storm was supernatural, but their appeals to all the gods they could think of went unheeded. They probably suspected that the crisis had something to do with the withdrawn stranger called Jonah they are carrying. If so those suspicions appear justified when they throw lots and Jonah is singled out as the culprit. The finger points ever more strongly at him when he tells the sailors with undisguised pride that he serves Jehovah, the God who created the sea (v. 9). Any lingering doubt is finally removed by Jonah's admittance in verse 10 that he is on the run from this God.

So the final question in this interrogation is inevitable: 'What shall we do to you?' Something has to be done and something has to be done to Jonah. That much is clear—but what? Jonah, as the prophet of the Lord, is uniquely qualified to say what the Lord requires. He does not hesitate: 'Pick me up and throw me in to the sea,' he says (v. 12).

Could Jonah have jumped?

Did they have to throw him in? Could Jonah not jump in himself? After all, he had brought such devastation to the ship and its crew already—surely it was a step too far to implicate them all in manslaughter? Perhaps it was, but there again Jonah could presumably have told them to turn the ship round and head back to Joppa since that was the way of obedience. That would have brought an end to the storm. Death was only the logical outcome because Jonah insisted on continuing on the road that led there.

But all of this is to speculate. Men made their choices and what happened, happened. Through it all God provides a remarkable picture for us. Jonah was to lodge in the belly of the great fish for three days and three nights, a poignant reminder of the Son of God lying in the tomb at Calvary (Matt. 12:40). From the sailors' point of view, their only hope of salvation lay in Jonah's death, the one dying for the many. By grabbing Jonah and throwing him overboard, they were necessarily implicated in his death. So too the many for whom Jesus Christ died are necessarily implicated in his death. Their life depends upon his death.

In addition, the act of picking Jonah up and throwing him in would meet with their idea of a fearful God whose anger had to be appeased. God would see this act of sacrifice on their part and his wrath would subside.

Seeking an alternative (v. 13)

The answer seemed so simple as far as the sailors were concerned. One brief moment and it could all be over. If they felt any later pangs of conscience about abandoning Jonah to the elements, they could always tell themselves that it was he who had told them to do it. But they were troubled at Jonah's advice. How could they be sure this would mean an end to Jehovah's hostilities? If Jonah's reluctance to go to Nineveh had stirred this God into directing such a violent storm at their boat, what hope was there for them if they conspired together to murder his prophet? Their natural anxiety for their own safety had showed itself in the final question they put to Jonah in verse 11—'What should we do to you to make the sea calm down *for us*?' [italics mine] But even so, it is possible that there was a genuine concern for Jonah. If so, it stood in marked contrast to Jonah's concern both for them and for the foreigners he would shortly be meeting in Nineveh.

And so these sailors bent their backs into rowing for the shore. In the Hebrew, the sense is that they dug deep. The oars ploughed deep into the foaming waves as the men summoned up what remaining energy and strength was left. But it was all futile. In fact, it made matters worse for 'the sea grew wilder than before'. Their actions were actually provocative. They were taking on Jehovah, the God of heaven, who made the sea and the land (v. 9) and this could never be an even contest.

> The tranquility that was to descend upon the Mediterranean would symbolize the peace that would exist between these sailors who sought forgiveness and the Lord who forgave them.

The little expression 'but they could not' which stands against these men's seemingly admirable efforts to save themselves and Jonah also stands against all man's attempts to save himself. All the expertise and strength of man is futile in assuaging the wrath of God. At one level, Jonah's words in verse 12 telling them to 'pick me up and throw me into the sea' is the last cry of a desperate man, weary of life but obstinate to the last in maintaining his stubborn disobedience. But, at an altogether different level, he speaks as the prophet of the Lord. Although he does not realize it, Jonah is playing the lead role in a drama which will serve as a little cameo of Calvary.

It comes down to this: these men are facing the wrath of God. Death appears certain, and all their best efforts to save themselves are doomed. Their single remaining hope is the death of Jonah—a solution which comes from the Lord via his prophet. If he dies, they live.

Seeking Forgiveness (v. 14)

Before they commit the deed, they commit themselves to prayer. When the storm first broke in verse 5 we find them desperately crying out to their pagan idols. As the events of the chapter have unfolded, those idols have been abandoned. It is Jonah's God to whom they now pray.

They plead with the Lord not to blame them for what they are about to do—take Jonah's life. Usually we ask forgiveness after sinning. Here the request is ahead of time. Their cry is that they have done their best to avoid sacrificing Jonah to the waves, but they are left with no other choice. God has been fighting against them and they have lost. Ultimately it has all proved hopeless—'for you, O LORD, have done as you pleased.'

God's answer did not come in words but in action. They did not die. The tranquility that was to descend upon the Mediterranean would symbolize the peace that would exist between these sailors who sought forgiveness and the Lord who forgave them. The meeting ground between them would be Jonah's watery grave.

An act of faith (v. 15)

Taking Jonah and throwing him overboard may have been all that was left to the sailors, but it was still an act of faith. There could be no going back now. Not only were they casting Jonah into the deep, but they were casting themselves upon God at the same time. There must have been immense anxiety among them as they tossed Jonah over the side. Would God answer their prayer not to hold them accountable for Jonah's life?

They did not have to wait long. The raging sea grew calm the instant Jonah hit the water. Behind the scenes God had spoken to the storm—a foretaste of the same obedience the wind and the waves would show to the Jesus Christ when he commanded them to be still in Mark 4:39. Like the waves, their anxiety could subside—God had evidently heard their prayers.

There is symmetry in the narrative. It began in verse 4 where God hurled a great wind upon the water and a violent storm arose. As we come full circle the sailors hurl Jonah into the water and the storm immediately subsides.

Seeking the Lord himself (v. 16)

Throughout chapter 1 the fear of the sailors has grown. It is a steady progression, not merely in intensity but in the focus of its direction. In verse 5 they are afraid at the storm. In verse 10 they are terrified at their plight as they realize from Jonah's answer that, in the storm, they have come face to face with Jehovah. But at the point where the sea becomes as flat as a mill-pond and it would appear the crisis is over, they are seized with a very great fear. This time it is for the Lord himself. They are not seeking something from him; they are seeking him.

Without apparently waiting until the ship finally limps home, they offer a sacrifice and make their vows. The sacrifice points back to the experience from which they have been delivered and it is offered in deep gratitude. The vows look ahead to what is to come as they promise to serve the Lord. Their experience is nothing less than a wholehearted conversion, having abandoned their idols during the course of the storm, and sought the face of Jehovah as the turbulent waters are subdued.

Serendipity (v. 17)

The Lord is always greater than the one we seek. As the sea closes over Jonah, there is every reason to think that the chapter has closed. But hidden from view, a great fish has been commissioned by the Lord, its appointed task being to swallow Jonah as he sinks into eternity.

God does not leave Jonah in the deep. He has been chasing a runaway, but now that he has caught him, the plan is far greater than punishing him. Certainly Jonah's experience is unpleasant and humbling, but God's purposes are essentially restorative rather than punitive. We see Jonah's restoration in what follows.

For further study ▶

1. Look at Mark 4:35-41 and compare the reaction of the disciples after the Lord had calmed the storm to the reaction of the sailors in Jonah 1:16. Why do you think there was this reaction when you might expect the serenity of a still evening's sunset to descend upon them?

2. On seeking the Lord, see Isaiah 55:6-7. Consider the difference between seeking the Lord and seeking things from the Lord.

TO THINK ABOUT AND DISCUSS

1. Consider the poor and compromised example of obedience and service that Jonah set before the sailors. Yet they were still drawn to the God Jonah purported to serve.

2. In many ways Jonah was the most successful prophet of the Old Testament. He preached and people were saved. He was also an exception to the general rule Stephen referred to in Acts 7:52. The irony is that he would have preferred to be like most of the other prophets whose call to repent and turn to the Lord was rejected and whose prophecies of impending judgement were fulfilled. What does this say about measuring God's servants by the success or failure they encounter?

3. The sailors do not see what is happening below the surface. God's purposes, and to some extent, the fullness of his gracious character, are hidden from their view. Maybe they will never know the story as we read it. What can we learn from this when God's purposes might be difficult to discern?

5 Out of the depths

(2:1-7)

One of the things you often notice about Bible characters is their utter honesty. There is none of the genteel and respectable masking of inner feelings. The superficial politeness of our culture would have been utterly foreign to them, as perhaps it should be to us. Not that we should always wear our hearts on our sleeves, but there is a point at which natural or cultural reserve crosses over into outright deception.

It was not a problem with the ancients, however. So when they were enraptured with the goodness of the Lord, they exploded into praise. And when they were in the depths, they said so. Nowhere is this clearer than in the book of Psalms. In fact, words from the Psalms were often the outlet for an individual bringing his or her praise, anxieties, despairs, frustrations and longings before the Lord. Whatever the human emotion, there was a Psalm or an extract to give it voice, and through which God could be addressed.

It explains why much of what Jonah said from inside the belly of the whale can be found in the Psalms. Words memorized from youth would find a ready expression as he poured out his heart to the Lord. With Jonah there was an added dimension. When the psalmist said that 'all your waves and breakers have swept over me' (Ps. 42:7), he meant it metaphorically, thinking of the immense pressures of life. When Jonah came to repeat those words, he meant it quite literally. Again, we know what the psalmist meant when he said that he cried to the Lord from the depths (Ps. 130:1), but when Jonah prayed that same prayer, he really was in the depths.

The great fish

Some people say that the story of Jonah is an allegory or a myth, rather like one of Aesop's fables. But there are solid reasons for taking the book as literal truth. For a start, Jonah was an historical character. Also the book is written as narrative and not in a style that would allow us to treat it as a parable. And, if the details are meant to represent something else, what is it? When we read of Jonah running away, are we supposed to think of Jonah running away but not necessarily by sea? Or when God hounds Jonah's steps by sending the storm and then saving him by sending a great fish, should we be thinking of God achieving his purposes in some other way? If so, why not just tell us how Jonah really did run away and how God went after him? If it was all a raging battle that was entirely limited to Jonah's mind and heart, the Bible is quite capable of conveying that to its readers. The conversation between Job and his friends did not need a dramatic setting to make its message understandable.

So when we read of a great fish swallowing Jonah, it is as well to accept it at face value. And then from inside the stomach of the fish, Jonah prays. Apart from the opening and closing verses, chapter 2 is entirely prayer—quite a change from Jonah's silence before God in chapter 1.

We should note that the fish is appointed by God. Even down to its precise placement within the Mediterranean Sea and the opening of its mouth, its every movement is directed by the Lord.

In the Bible the monster of the deep is a great symbol of evil living in the untamed waters of sinful chaos. It may be that the Lord intends us to see that such great forces are ultimately in his hands and cannot move without his say-so. More than that, even when individual Christians seem to be swallowed up by something far greater and more powerful than themselves, they must know that they are not out of God's reach. In a few years the nation of Israel would be gobbled up by the evil monster of Assyria, with its capital Nineveh—the very people to whom Jonah had been appointed to go. There are two important lessons Israel should understand ahead of time: first, that Assyria, or any other world power, does not operate other than at God's express direction; and second, that even from the stomach of evil, God hears the cries of his penitent people.

Jonah's prayer

Although Jonah prays from inside the fish it is not his first prayer. His first prayer came as he was tossed into the water. He had gone down to Joppa, down to the ship, down into its hold, and then finally he sank down and down in the sea. It was not the horror of drowning that terrified him, but the thought of being abandoned by the Lord in death. Despite his long and determined flight from the presence of God, the prospect of ending his life outside the presence of God, and then for ever, are too terrifying for words. And so, as the final seconds of his fragile life approached, he cried out in immense distress to the Lord, *his* God (despite Jonah's disobedience he had never stopped looking upon the Lord as his God). In the desperation of that cry the Lord answered and rescued him. The Lord provided a great fish to swallow Jonah (1:17). Suddenly Jonah is snatched violently and thrown headlong into a hot and constricted mass of rotting vegetable matter. Through the utter confusion of what is happening to him, he eventually comes round and realizes that he can breathe—after a fashion. And then it dawns on him what has happened. The Lord has answered his prayer for deliverance!

> Despite his long and determined flight from the presence of God, the prospect of ending his life outside the presence of God, and then for ever, are too terrifying for words.

So now, from inside the fish, Jonah reflects on what has just happened to him. His prayer is one of thankfulness and hope. It is also full of description as he recalls the extremity of his plight. From the depths he had cried and from the depths he had been heard. Quite rightly, he does not blame the sailors for throwing him into the water but sees that the Lord has been behind all of it ('You hurled me into the deep', v. 3). Jonah acknowledges that he had been sinking down—a process that had begun before he even got to Joppa in 1:3. The self-induced downward slide had brought him to the very gateway of death. He describes himself as being at the depths of the grave, but the Lord his God had brought his 'life up from the pit' (v. 6).

Hope

Inside the great fish the heat , the overpoweringly nauseous smell and the burning of the stomach acids must have been horrific. Maybe Jonah was slipping in and out of consciousness and alludes to it in verse 7, 'When my life was ebbing away, I remembered you, Lord.' But there is hope here. The Lord who has saved him so dramatically from the water will surely deliver him at last. Jonah could have confidence that the Lord who had answered this initial prayer would bring him final deliverance (v. 4). He would yet sing praises of thanksgiving (v. 9a) and would return to useful service (v. 9b). Jonah would have agreed with John Newton when he wrote:

> And can He have taught me
> To trust in His Name,
> And thus far have brought me
> To put me to shame.

The Lord's answer

Jonah's prayer went straight into the Lord's dwelling place (v. 7). From there the Lord answered him (v. 2). Not only was this in stark contrast to the pagan idols who had been impotent to answer the desperate pleas of the sailors, but it was also in complete contrast to Jonah himself who had turned a consistently deaf ear to the Lord throughout chapter 1.

But we should note that while Jonah's first prayer, from the depths of the sea, was answered spectacularly and immediately, as indeed it had to be, his second prayer from within the fish was answered after a considerably long time. It was to be three long days before Jonah would finally be delivered. We can only speculate what went through his mind during that period. He had no way of measuring time, of course, but it must have seemed endless. Certainly, when it eventually ended it is likely that Jonah was physically incapable of lasting very much longer.

So why did the Lord not answer sooner? Why did Jonah's ordeal have to be so drawn out? Surely he had learnt his lesson and was now ready to serve him. That ought to have been the Lord's cue to step in and rescue Jonah, we would think. Instead the awful thought was growing in Jonah's mind that he had been abandoned by God in the gateway to the eternity of hell. Jonah must have asked himself repeatedly: 'Will this experience of Sheol (or hell) never end?'

Jonah probably lived the remainder of his life wondering why God had left him for such a long time before answering his prayer. It is significant that he took the trouble to find out just how long he had been inside the fish and then record it in his narrative. In doing so, we have an insight into God's purposes here—a purpose which is wrapped up in redemptive history. Jonah's experience would be a visual aid for the disbelieving Jews in Jesus' day. Anxious to see a sign, the Son of Man would give them just one—'the sign of the prophet Jonah' (Matt. 12:38-41). After his death and burial Jesus would be in the heart of the earth for the same length of time as Jonah had been in the belly of the great fish—three days.

In other words, there *was* a purpose to the three days, even if Jonah never learned what it was. The initial swallowing of Jonah and his eventual discharge on to the beach were in divine hands. But so too was everything else that occurred, including the elapse of time between those two events. With the benefit of hindsight we can see the purposes of God coming to pass even though it meant that Jonah's pleas for deliverance from the fish were not answered immediately.

For further study ▶

FOR FURTHER STUDY

1. Look at Psalm 139:7-8: 'Where can I go from your Spirit? Where can I flee from your presence? If I go up to heaven, you are there; if I make my bed in the depths, you are there.' In what ways would Jonah have agreed with these words?

2. Read Psalm 130. What is the evidence that the psalmist is not just thinking of the depths of overwhelming circumstances, but also of self-inflicted troubles and misery?

TO THINK ABOUT AND DISCUSS

1. The church can sometimes seem very weak and vulnerable, even to the point of being swallowed up by modern day monsters such as secularism, materialism and other religions. What does this passage show us?

2. Consider Jonah's prayer. It mostly describes his anguish. Does he actually ask God for anything in these verses? What is important—the actual words used or what lies behind them? Compare them with the fine words Jonah uses in 1:9.

3. What do these verses tell us about the value of learning verses and portions of Scripture by heart?

4. What do we learn from this passage about unanswered prayer and the ultimate purposes of God?

6 Salvation comes from the Lord

(2:8-10)

It is only when Jonah is treading the very doorstep to death that he finally turns to the Lord. No one could be a more fitting candidate as patron saint of people who leave things to the last minute. In his own words, it is from the belly of Sheol that he cries out to the Lord. Even though his anguish and plight have been self-inflicted, the Lord hears him and answers his prayer.

His prayer in the water is answered instantaneously, but the dark night of despair inside the fish drags on and on before God's reply is received. Nonetheless the Lord had a purpose in prolonging Jonah's stay in the fish. And so, at the right time, he is violently thrown up on the beach.

The words of Jonah's prayer in chapter 2 seem to be very eloquently expressed. But the reality may have been somewhat different. More probably they were gasped in brief snatches of barely-conscious awareness of where he was and what was happening. Only upon his ultimate escape from the horrors of this chapter does he reflect on it all. And then, in a calmer moment, he commits his prayers, cries and emotions to writing.

In verses 8 and 9, even though the ordeal continues, Jonah reflects back and gives us the lesson he has learned thus far. He also states his resolve with regard to the future. It is a pivotal moment in his experience. It is the point at which the Lord speaks to the fish and gets it to release its distressed victim. It is as though the Lord has been waiting to hear these words from his servant. Now that it has arrived, there is no need to detain Jonah further—he's ready for the next stage. And so, since this is the lesson the Lord has been at such pains to teach Jonah, and since it was such a hard-fought lesson to teach, it would pay us well to consider it carefully.

'Those who cling to worthless idols'

The lesson Jonah learnt went far deeper than a mere contrast between the Lord who had answered prayer and the pagan idols who had been deaf to the cries of the helpless sailors in chapter 1. It was not about the idols as such, but about those who make time for them and pay them regard. The NIV puts it more strongly—referring to those who cling to them. The Lord himself says that he is not provoked to jealousy by idols (for they are nothing), but by their adherents. When he says in Deuteronomy 32:21 that they have 'angered me with their worthless idols', he is complaining about his own people who pander after idols.

Who does Jonah mean here when he speaks of 'those who

cling to worthless idols'? Is he thinking of the sailors? Possibly. Certainly the force of his personal statement in verse 9 suggests a contrast between himself and idolaters. If this is right, his assessment of the ship's crew is hopelessly adrift. By the time Jonah had been hurled into the sea, they had long abandoned their former idols. Even as he was praying from the horrors of his plight, they were offering their sacrifices to the Lord and making vows to him (1:16). Jonah was promising to do the same (2:9), but the sailors were actually ahead of him.

When Jonah had been in the ship with the sailors he had acted in a very aloof manner. Even now there may have been a trace of smug hypocrisy still remaining, although probably not enough to warrant the comment from one of the commentators that even the fish was so sickened by Jonah's hypocritical piety that it threw up! Even at our best moments (and chapter 2 certainly sees Jonah at his best), we are shot through with flaws and failings. Moreover the fish vomited Jonah out when the Lord spoke to it (v. 10) and not when it heard Jonah.

'Forfeit the grace that could be theirs'

The phrase 'forfeit the grace that could be theirs' could be translated in a number of different ways. Literally, it means 'forsake loyalty'. This could be a comment upon abandoning the steadfast loyalty of God himself, the loving and faithful friend. Or it could mean the individual's personal loyalty to the idols. In other words, those who cling to worthless idols will eventually see them for what they are and will be forced to desert them.

It is worth considering these words. Jonah has been reflecting upon the folly of his attempt to run from the presence of the Lord. His dark and painful experience has brought him to his senses. He may well be thinking of himself in verse 8 and his reckless disloyalty, since he had certainly abandoned the Lord.

Equally, it could mean that Jonah was forced to abandon his idols. Admittedly, he had not been worshipping a pagan idol as the sailors had, but his dream of pursuing a new life away from God in Tarshish was just as idolatrous. He was also in danger of making an idol out of national Israel and elevating it above the purposes of God. His refusal to obey God in chapter 1 arose through an unwillingness to embrace the possibility that the Lord could care enough about other people to extend his grace to them. So he clung to his world view that the Lord would only ever bless Israelites and only ever condemn non-Israelites. Nothing seemed to shake him from this dogma—he was still clinging on when the sailors threw him overboard. Only when in the water, and with mere seconds of his earthly life remaining, does he finally let go. It is possible to understand Jonah as saying that, just as had happened in his own case, God will ultimately prise every

> The sailors were perishing in 1:6, Jonah was perishing in 2:6 and the Ninevites were perishing in 3:9. Yet each in turn was brought back from the brink and found salvation. And that salvation was found only in the Lord.

finger away from the object of its love. One day every idol will lie abandoned.

Clinging on

But it isn't enough to let go of the idols. We only have one set of hands. The question is—what are we going to cling to instead? The humanist believes that man should not be in the business of clinging to anything or anyone. 'This is life,' he says. 'Just get on with it.'

The Christian response is that it is not a matter of finding a helpful crutch to lean on and help us through life. Rather, man is in an absolutely desperate situation—he is perishing. The sailors were perishing in 1:6, Jonah was perishing in 2:6 and the Ninevites were perishing in 3:9. Yet each in turn was brought back from the brink and found salvation. And that salvation was found only in the Lord—hence the need to cling to him alone, the sole author of salvation. The Christian gospel is unchanged through the centuries. Man is still perishing and God is still saving those who cling to Jesus Christ, the only Saviour for sinners.

The experience of all those who believes in Jesus is that just as they think they are clinging on to him, he is in fact clinging on to them and holding them up.

Jonah's commitment

There were two aspects to Jonah's commitment. First, he says that he will sacrifice to the Lord. He is referring to ongoing acts of worship and not a one-off. He also says that he will do so with a song of thanksgiving. He knows only too well that previous duties have been undertaken with a sullen and grudging attitude—the Lord deserves far better than that.

Second, he says that he will make good what he has vowed. The sacrifices look back to past mercies; the vows look forward to future service. Did he mean them? Yes, he did. Did he keep them? Sadly, no. In chapter 4 he slips back into his old resentful response to the idea that undeserving people of other nations should taste God's grace.

The important point here is not so much Jonah's commitment to the Lord but the Lord's commitment to Jonah. Jonah meant well as he made his promises, but God knew him inside out. He was a very long way from what he should be and the Lord had not finished with him. The lesson of salvation is not merely that God's grace is made available in the initial act of deliverance. There is the ongoing lesson of God's persevering grace, teaching and disciplining wayward and headstrong servants like Jonah. This is the work of a lifetime. There is a sense in which they will never be fit for the Master's service, but that does not stop the Lord's continuing work of moulding and shaping his servants.

Jonah's confession

Jonah's confession comes in verse 9. He says: 'Salvation comes from the LORD.'

Spurgeon says that he 'learned this good sentence of theology in a strange college.' It was not gleaned from a Bible College or a good book, but rather this truth had been chiselled into his heart from his own traumatic experience. Utterly unable to save himself, Jonah had come to see that from beginning to end, saving the perishing was God's unique work.

Deliverance

When he finally got hold of this truth and said these words, we have the miracle of verse 10—the fish vomited Jonah up on to the dry land. It marks Jonah's final deliverance. As the fish disgorges its human occupant we observe that death has been swallowed up by grace.

The miracle consists in the remarkable positioning of the fish in the shallow waters near the beach—anywhere else and Jonah, in his semi-conscious condition, would certainly have drowned.

Jonah will come round from the nightmare of the past three days and receive a new commissioning from the Lord. The lessons he has learned are about to be put to the test.

For further study ▶

FOR FURTHER STUDY

1. Consider Psalm139:1-10. The psalmist has sought to run from the Lord but has come to realize what a foolish notion that is. In verse 8 he says that if he makes his bed in the depths (or in Sheol—the place of the dead), the Lord is there. Consider Jonah's determination to undertake his journey of defiance which will only end as he approaches the bottom of the sea. It is his choice to make his bed here. Yet notice the surprise. Anyone would expect to find the Lord in the heavens, but not here.

2. Consider John 3:13-21. This passage explains that God's salvation is achieved through his Son, Jesus Christ, who was lifted up on a cross so that everyone who believes in him may have eternal life. The same hope expressed by the ship's captain in 1:6 and by Nineveh's king in 3:9 that Jonah's God would not let them perish is held out for us as an absolute promise for us by God in John 3:16.

3. In John 6:44-60 Jesus is unafraid to tell his listeners that no one will ever seek salvation in him unless that person is drawn by the Father. It is because of our innate helplessness to save ourselves that we can only cry out to God himself to save us.

TO THINK ABOUT AND DISCUSS

1. If Jonah was thinking of himself and his patriotic love for his own nation in verse 8, he is admitting that it is possible to make an idol out of *good* things rather than the Lord himself. What good things can become idols and how?

2. In Genesis 32:22-32 Jacob wrestled with the Lord and clung on to him. Think about the words 'cling to' and consider what it means to cling to worthless idols and then cling to the living God.

3. Perhaps Jonah was thinking ahead to the Ninevites when he referred to those who cling to worthless idols. Certainly the Ninevites worshipped many gods. Looking ahead to chapter 3 and the repentance of Nineveh, what did it take to get the fingers of the countless hands that clung to these idols to release their hold upon them?

7 Ground-hog day

(3:1-5)

Chapter 3 represents Jonah's 'ground-hog day'—a chance at a re-run of that monumentally significant day when he began the long defiant walk from his home in Gath-hepher, headed for the port of Joppa (1:3) and kept on going. Now God speaks again.

This time, his word to Jonah is met with full-hearted obedience. Jonah takes an even longer walk to Nineveh where his warning of judgement is embraced as the word of God. Throughout the city the universal response is one of repentance, leading to the staying of God's hand in judgement.

Another chance

The word of the Lord comes to Jonah a second time (v. 1). Jonah was not the first servant of the Lord to have been given another chance. He will not be the last. The words of Jesus in Matthew 12:20 that the Lord's anointed servant (i.e. Jesus himself) will not break a bruised reed or snuff out a smouldering wick, indicate that it is God's habit not to discard those who fail him. Wind instrumentalists blow through a reed. If damaged in any way, it leads to a dull hollow sound. For all practical purposes a bruised reed is worthless and easily replaced. So too is flax which, when damp, only billows out smoke and never ignites. In either case the obvious remedy is the easiest—give up and start again. But the Lord refuses to break the bruised reed or quench the smoking flax. He does not drop team members who let him, and

> So Jonah is in exactly the position he was in before— the only change being in Jonah himself. He has been to the depths, wiped his feet on the welcome-mat of the grave and returned.

the rest of the team, down. He does not *have* to use Jonah but chooses to do so. In fact he delights to build up his church with what would otherwise be rejects.

We do not know how long Jonah had to recuperate from his experiences. However, the urgency of the situation and the pace of the narrative indicate minimal delay. The Lord speaks—Jonah gets up and goes.

The task (vv. 1-2)

There are so many ways in which the Lord could have spoken to Jonah. He could have reminded him of the disasters surrounding the first commissioning. The Lord could have warned him that he was about to get one last chance to prove himself. He could have reminded him of his vow in 2:9. Or he could have sought to persuade him of the benefits of obedience and the need for Nineveh to hear the message.

Instead, the Lord simply tells Jonah to go—to the same place, to the same people and with the same urgency. After all, the wickedness of the Ninevites has not abated. On the other hand, the mercy of God in forgiveness has not relented either. Jonah must go with the same God-given message; he is not free to add to it, embellish it or soften it in any way. Neither is he to change his style. There is no difference between the 'proclaim to it' in 3:2 and the 'preach against it' in 1:2. Their wickedness continues to come up before the Lord, and Jonah must cry out against it. The task is therefore every bit as demanding as the first time around. It still means taking up his cross and following his Lord.

So Jonah is in exactly the position he was in before—the only change being in Jonah himself. He has been to the depths, wiped his feet on the welcome-mat of the grave and returned. Jonah is not the same man—how could he be?

Jonah's response (vv. 3-4)

The last time Jonah had heard the word of the Lord, he got up and made a run for it—in the opposite direction. This time he obeys. He has made his vows (2:9) and intends to keep them. On the previous occasion, the destination (Tarshish) was irrelevant and the focus centred entirely upon the journey. This time the destination (Nineveh) is all-important and the journey, even though it would have been quite an undertaking at 900 miles, is not mentioned.

Again we are told that Nineveh is a great or important city

(1:2; 3:3). It was great in its own eyes and therefore suffered from the guilt of pride. It was also great in the eyes of its enemies and hence their reaction of fear. But more than that, it was also great in the eyes of God. Its greatness in wickedness drew the wrath of God, but its size, importance and unknowing helplessness also drew his compassion (4:11). The Lord cared about great Nineveh. That is why he sent Jonah.

A three-day journey

In the description of the size of Nineveh we are told that it was a city of three days' journey. Commentators take different views as to what this might mean. Some say it refers to the time it would take to circumnavigate the entire city. Others take it to mean that a thorough visit to every part of the city would take three days. Some believe that the days come from the first day of arrival, the second day of the visit proper and the third day of departure. A more recent view is that it comes from the appropriate period of protocol given to a foreign guest visiting an important city. In some ways it does not matter. We are told repeatedly throughout the book that Nineveh was great. This is the writer's way of saying just how big the city was.

But we ought to consider the possibility that the Lord intends us to see something else here. Mention three days in the context of Jonah, and we immediately recall his three days inside the fish. Are we intended to draw some conclusions from that connection perhaps? It could be, for instance, that the Lord is telling us that, although disobedience may lead us to the threshold of death and the feeling of abandonment by the Lord, so too might obedience. Jonah had spent three days in the place of God's judgement; now he must go another three days to rescue others who are also under God's judgement. For Jonah, both experiences were unwelcome, but the Lord brought him through them.

The message

Jonah's message was extremely short. As he began on the first day of his street walk towards the centre of Nineveh, he just repeated over and over: 'Forty more days and Nineveh will be overturned.' Many people think Jonah must have said a lot more which is not recorded. Doubtless he did, but it may have been that he simply answered the natural questions fired at him from people whose consciences had been stirred. They would have been anxious to find out about this God who was threatening them. And what had they done specifically which had angered him so? What could they do to assuage his wrath? The situation demanded answers.

Clearly the message that Nineveh would be overthrown was a devastating one. It was a solemn message of impending judgement and suggested that something cataclysmic would shortly befall them. This was the issue at the heart of Jonah's grievance. He had prophesied destruction and would only be happy if it came to pass. However, the word translated 'overthrown' can also mean 'turn upside down'. In other words, if Nineveh experienced a complete and radical change of heart she could legitimately be described as having been 'overthrown'. This is of course precisely what happened.

The embodiment of the message

There is an account of a man who survived being swallowed by a sperm whale in 1891, although some doubt has been cast upon its authenticity. Initially thought to have been lost at sea in a whaling accident, James Bartley was discovered when the whale was caught and cut open a couple of days later. He was pulled from the stomach unconscious but he came round and eventually resumed his life as a whaler. The significant aspect of the account is that for the rest of his life he was strangely bleached. Considering he had lain in the gastric acids of the whale's stomach at temperatures of around 105°F it is hardly surprising.

It is not unreasonable to think that Jonah was similarly bleached. If so, it is difficult to imagine people holding back from the inevitable question: 'What happened to you?' His story would then unfold as a living example of the truth he proclaimed. Even if this is pure conjecture, it is nonetheless true that Jonah himself was a living embodiment of his message. Both Jonah and the Ninevites had wilfully ignored God's word to them (although in the case of the Ninevites the voice of God came indirectly to them through their consciences). Both Jonah and the Ninevites, as a consequence, faced the imminent judgement of the Lord. Jonah could tell them that he had

> In a single movement they turned their backs upon their old way of life and turned their faces in hope to the God of mercy.

duly turned from his sin and cried out to the Lord. There was no need to explain his deliverance and restoration in detail—that much was self-evident. The personal testimony of Jonah and the message he declared were all of a piece, both aspects reinforcing the other in a powerful plea to the Ninevites to repent and turn to the living God.

The Ninevites' response (v. 5)

Verse 5 is a key moment in the book, just as 2:1 had been a key moment for Jonah ('from inside the fish Jonah prayed'). Although it was obvious that the Ninevites believed what Jonah was telling them about their city being overthrown, this is not how it is recorded. Rather, we are told that they believed God. They took Jonah to be a faithful prophet and embraced the message he was bringing them from the Lord. It was God's message they heard and God's message they believed.

However 'believing God' goes deeper than just believing what they had been told. It also means that they believed *in* God. They were not merely heeding his warning but were casting themselves upon him. The declaration of a fast and the wearing of sackcloth was an outward expression reflecting a genuine and heartfelt turning away from sin. But the fact that they believed in God indicates that the 'turning away' was matched by a 'turning to' at the same time. In a single movement they turned their backs upon their old way of life and turned their faces in hope to the God of mercy.

A fast is declared. It may have been little more than a formal recognition of what was already happening since they were grieving over their sin, and those who grieve do not feel like eating. They also put on sackcloth—thick coarse cloth, often made from goats' hair. It symbolized their inner self-abasement.

Jonah's preaching put a torch to the very fabric of Ninevite society. Once ignited, the flames swept all before it, engulfing every social group, from the greatest to the least. They were to reach to the palace itself, as we shall see.

FOR FURTHER STUDY

1. Consider Acts 17:1-7. In Thessalonica, Paul and Silas had reasoned with the Jews that Jesus was the Christ and that he had to suffer and die and then rise again. The message divided the hearers. Some were persuaded and joined the believers. But others stirred up trouble. Their complaint, in literal terms, was that Paul and Silas had turned the world upside down by their preaching (v. 6). Compare this with the threat that Nineveh would be overthrown.

2. Refer to Acts 20:21. Consider how repentance and faith represent the two aspects of 'turning from' and 'turning to'.

TO THINK ABOUT AND DISCUSS

1. If Jonah embodied the message he brought, how did Jesus Christ embody the message he brought? All believers are called upon to bear witness to their Saviour. How should that be done?

2. See Matthew 12:38-41. We are invited to make comparisons here. First, how does Jonah's experience in the fish parallel that of Jesus Christ, the Son of Man? Second, compare the character of Jonah and his preaching with that of Jesus and his preaching. Third, compare the response of the Ninevites with that of the men and women of Jesus' day.

3. In view of the response Jesus encountered in his day, what does that tell us about the response of people in general and the causes of it?

8 All change

(3:6-10)

Has there ever been a revival which swept up a community quite so universally as Nineveh under the preaching of Jonah? From all quarters of the social spectrum, people were gripped with shame and sorrow for their sin. Turning from it, they cried out to God. And when God saw it he had compassion on them and lifted his threat of destruction (v. 10). By some, it has been described as the greatest revival in world history, although others would disagree.

A surprising outcome

Nineveh's reaction to Jonah was all the more remarkable because the message itself seemed so absurd. One strange-looking foreigner standing in front of a towering wall repeating endlessly that the city would be overturned in forty days invited mockery. Who could possibly overturn Nineveh? In any normal circumstances Jonah would, at best, have been laughed out of town or ignored as a mad fool. At the same time, he could have expected persecution or even execution. Certainly other prophets had met their death for lesser predictions in less hostile surroundings.

And if the repentance of Nineveh was remarkable because the message appeared far-fetched, it was even more surprising when you consider the messenger—Jonah himself.

Despite the outward obedience in chapter 3 to God's directive to go to Nineveh and preach (v. 1), it is difficult to think that his heart was entirely in it. While his actions in this chapter stand in marked contrast to the disobedience of chapter 1 and the brooding petulance of chapter 4, it is too much to expect that he preached—as Richard Baxter did in the England of the seventeenth century—'as a dying man to dying men'. His mission was to go to Nineveh and preach. He was not told to care about the Ninevites. He would do his duty and go home. Yet the Ninevites believed the prophet of God. More than that, they believed the God of the prophet (v. 5).

The king of Nineveh

In verse 6 we are told that the news reached the king of Nineveh. Perhaps he was aloof from many of the everyday events in the capital, but Nineveh had been gripped by something so momentous that it was only a matter of time before some of the gossip filtered through to him. He may have insisted on hearing the whole story from beginning to end.

The king could have reacted in a number of different ways.

The actions of the people in declaring a fast and putting on sackcloth were so widespread that, to an onlooker, it must have appeared organized. It could easily have been interpreted as the work of seditious forces: a strange and potentially dangerous movement afoot; the threat of civil unrest; something to be stamped upon before it spread any further. And this was particularly so when a public outpouring of grief at their violent and cruel ways looked very much like a rebellion against Assyrian foreign policy. We could expect the king to view it as the prelude to a popular uprising and deal with it with customary brutality. But no.

He could have decided to sit it out until the emotion had passed. Perhaps too he could have sought to harness the city-wide outpouring of grief to his own ends in some way—adopt a sympathetic and populist approach that would endear him to the people and serve as an early example in political expediency. None of these options is taken. Instead he is affected in precisely the same way as the people.

The king's repentance (v. 6)

There is a neat symmetry to the king's response in verse 6. He gets up, takes off, puts on and sits down. It is a remarkable act in its spontaneous humility and repentance. He arises from the throne, removes his royal robes, puts on sackcloth and sits down in the dust. In one sense, it was a simple gesture not requiring a great deal of energy and probably not taking him very far geographically. In another sense, it cost him everything and a single step equated with a period of light years. In a matter of minutes he had personally taken himself from the top of society and placed himself deliberately at its very bottom. Ashes speak of fire and judgement; dust speaks of the end of all men. The king is saying that, despite his earthly privileges, it is among the dust of death that he rightly belongs. Such an act and such a statement was all the more astonishing for the fact that he only heard the word of God second hand.

The king's decree (vv. 7-8)

Having set the example in a spontaneous act of personal self-abasement, the king and the nobles together issue a decree requiring the citizens of Nineveh to do exactly the same, i.e. repent from their sin and call upon God. In point of fact the people are some way ahead of him at this stage. They are already in sackcloth by the time he gets to

> The king gets up, takes off, puts on and sits down. It is a remarkable act in its spontaneous humility and repentance.

hear the news. It is not clear that he is telling them to do anything which they have not already done, or are doing. Nonetheless, his decree gives a focus and leadership to the crisis at hand and his personal example gives it added force.

Even if the people have not quite grasped the significance of the forty days, the king has. He therefore tells everyone to call urgently on God. The king understands that there is no sense in God giving them a forty-day warning period if there is not some chance, however slight, of him relenting. The question is—what would make him relent? Well, since his anger has been stoked up by their wickedness (1:2), they must show him that they are serious about renouncing their evil and violent ways.

There is a healthy partnership here between people and king. Had the king's decree been imposed without the people having been moved and troubled as the king had been, it would have achieved little. Surely the judgement would have fallen just as Jonah promised. Without a movement of God among the inhabitants of Nineveh, the result of the king's decree could never have got beyond an outward conformity to a law. And yet it needed the king to give a sense of direction to the nation's grief and impress upon the people that the need of the hour was not merely to turn from sin but to turn to the Lord himself. He therefore tells his people to call urgently on God.

Involvement of the animals (v. 8a)

By the king's decree, cattle and sheep were also to be deprived of food and water. They, of course, did not share in the guilt that invited God's judgement, but man and beast were bound together within the life of the community. The animals shared in the good times; they would suffer if harm came to their city and benefit if she was spared. It was therefore appropriate that the bellowing and bleating of distressed animals should mingle with the cries of the people as they sought God—one united voice ascending to the Lord, just as their wickedness had done (1:2).

Call urgently on God (v. 8b)

The king directed the people to plead with the Lord. He was right to do so. After all, the people had something to say to the Lord. It was far more important that they express the inner turmoil of their hearts in words than merely demonstrate the emotion of grief through the external signs of fasting and wearing sackcloth. Although God sees us, he particularly wants to hear us.

The sin of Nineveh was something in which the entire community shared. It was therefore appropriate that the entire community come together in repentance over it. Yet, sin is committed by individuals and each must carry the burden of his own sin. Knowing this, the king tells them that every one of them should personally turn from his own evil and violent ways. Again he is right. Man's sinfulness has an individual as well as a corporate dimension to it.

And so as the city wept for its sin, individuals also sought the Lord personally. Each person carried two burdensome weights to the Lord. One was in a package marked 'our sin'; the other in a package marked 'my sin'.

A shred of hope (v. 9)

The words of the king: 'Who knows? God may yet relent and with compassion turn from his fierce anger so that we will not perish' carry a vestige of hope. It may not be great, but it is all that he has and he will hang on to it. The same kind of desperate yet real faith is found in the captain's words to Jonah in 1:6 where he demands that Jonah call upon his God and comments: 'Maybe he will take notice of us and we will not perish.' The thought in both of these men is that if they turn from their sin, maybe God will turn from his wrath. And then, having turned from his wrath—dare they hope it—maybe he will turn to them.

The faint hope in God entertained by pagan men in this book is made absolutely certain in the light of New Testament truth. Both the king and the captain understand that without divine mercy they will certainly perish. The prayers they urge in desperation to be prayed are designed to avoid such an outcome, but it is impossible to avoid the feeling that they see this as their last and rapidly fading hope. However nobody praying that same prayer nowadays need approach God with such timidity. We have the famous words of John 3:16: 'For God so loved the world that he gave his one and only Son, that whoever believes in him shall not perish but have eternal life'. It is the death and resurrection of Jesus Christ which means that, with repentant hearts, we can pray the prayer that pagan Ninevites prayed and know with rock-solid confidence that we are forgiven for Christ's sake.

> I hear the words of love,
> I gaze upon the blood,
> I see the mighty sacrifice,
> And I have peace with God.
> (Horatius Bonar)

The Lord's response (v. 10)

There has been a change in the heart of the people and a change in the heart of the king. There is therefore a change in the heart of God. This is not repentance in the sense of regretting something done earlier, but God's response to a complete turnaround in Ninevite thinking and acting.

Judgement was lifted when God saw what they did and

how they turned from their evil ways. It was not when he saw their tears or observed their fasts. It was not even when he heard their cries to him. Although he could read their hearts, the threat of destruction was only removed in compassion when the Lord could see that their grief was genuine.

For further study ▶

FOR FURTHER STUDY

1. Read the book of Nahum. Within 150 years, Nineveh had abandoned the fruits of repentance and returned to her previous violence and wickedness. This time there is no repentance and the 'city of blood' (Nahum 3:1) is destroyed as prophesied. This does not mean that their repentance in Jonah 3:10 was not genuine. It was—Jesus said so (Matt. 12:41). However, it does show that a past act of repentance does not guarantee future safety. A return to sin needs a corresponding return to repentance.

2. See Daniel 4:28-37 and Acts 12:19-25 and compare the humility of the unnamed king of Nineveh with the pride of both Nebuchadnezzar and Herod. Note also how the Lord deals differently with each of them.

3. Look up Acts 20:21. Repentance and faith are two sides of the one coin called conversion. Consider how both are seen in Jonah 3.

TO THINK ABOUT AND DISCUSS

1. Refer to Matthew 5:13. Salt is pictured as a preservative, acting as a brake on society's downward slide into moral decay. Good laws or kingly directives (such as in Jonah 3:7-9) can do the same, although they cannot give life. Discuss the place and importance of such brakes.

2. Modern western society focuses its attention upon corporate sins such as rampant consumerism that leads to global warming. What does the repentance of the Ninevites teach us about personal responsibility?

3. What are the parallels between Nineveh's repentance and any individual conversion?

9 Where the mood takes you

(4:1-6)

In the space of a few verses, Jonah's mood-swings take him from Death Valley to Happy Mountain and back again. It is a bewildering journey that leaves him feeling useless and exhausted. It is also a journey on which the Lord accompanies him every step of the way.

With Jonah having finally gone to Nineveh and having preached the message entrusted to him, the Lord is not going to abandon him now that the mission is over. There is much Jonah needs to learn. He may be able to quote many of the Psalms with ease, but his understanding of the God of the Psalms seems woefully short. He also needs to grasp the value of a soul. Not least, he must learn to walk humbly with his Lord and not be led by feelings. In all of this, the Lord is his instructor.

If chapter 2 of the book records Jonah's response to his own deliverance, chapter 4 gives us Jonah's response to the deliverance of the Ninevites. The deep contrast between the moving psalmody of chapter 2 and the bitter complaint of chapter 4 speaks volumes—all to Jonah's shame.

Jonah's anger (vv 1, 2)

In verse 1, Jonah's anger boils over. It had been bubbling up inside him and now comes spilling out when he sees the Lord relenting from the threat of overthrowing Nineveh. It is a depressingly ugly mood. As the Lord turns from his anger at the close of chapter 3, so Jonah turns to his at the beginning of chapter 4. He was happy to be a prophet of doom but only so long as the doom was to occur. When God sees the repentance of Nineveh and lifts his threat of destruction, so Jonah lifts the shackles on his otherwise dormant emotions and gives full vent to them.

> It is not just a little irritation that Jonah feels—it is absolute fury. Literally 'it was evil to Jonah a great evil'. These are shocking words. It is one thing when people rail against God for troubles and calamities in life. Jonah's fury is different.

It is not just a little irritation that Jonah feels—it is absolute fury. Literally 'it was evil to Jonah a great evil'. These are shocking words. It is one thing when people rail against God for troubles and calamities in life. Jonah's fury is different. He is enraged that there is no calamity. He looks at the kindness and mercy of the Lord and calls it evil. For him, Nineveh had got away with it too easily. Even though their repentance had been genuine enough, surely their violence and immorality was so deep-seated and extreme that it merited some kind of punishment from God. Or so Jonah thinks. He does not use the words 'cheap grace' but that is what he means.

Jonah's prayer

His mood was black and his complaint was out of order but at least Jonah pours out his burden before the Lord. It was certainly better than running away. More than that, it was actually a good response. It is very easy to avoid prayer with the excuse that we need to wait until we feel more in the mood for it. But sometimes it is the very mood itself that needs to be brought before the Lord. There are many instances in Scripture where people are rebuked for their approach to the Lord, but it is usually because of self-righteousness and hypocrisy. We do not find those who genuinely wish to engage with God being turned away. We may cringe at the intemperateness of Jonah's outburst, but God himself seems perfectly at ease with it.

The effect of Jonah's mood

However, the fact that the Lord does not rebuke Jonah does not mean that his emotional state does not matter. It does. Moreover, Jonah must answer for it. We also see in these verses where Jonah's mood takes him. It is not a welcoming place.

(1) ISOLATION

Jonah is on his own (v. 5). We might well ask 'why?' It is clear from chapter 1 that Jonah is a bit of a 'loner'. He had more of an excuse on the ship since, on that occasion, he was among pagans. But here there is no such justification. There may be times when believers are called upon to battle it out alone, but it is not very often and it is not here.

Staying on in Nineveh would have been the obvious thing for Jonah to have done. Following the city-wide revival, he would have been among fellow believers in Jehovah, who needed to know more about the God before whom they had bowed. The Ninevites already appreciated Jonah for his part in bringing them God's word and would have provided an eager audience for him. But instead of exercising a useful ministry among these new converts, Jonah cuts himself off. His hostile mood to God's withdrawal of the threat of punishment has the inevitable effect of putting a distance between himself and the Ninevites. They have been the recipients of God's grace, but they are no friends of Jonah. It is Jonah's mood which means he wants nothing to do with them. Isolating himself in this way has led to useless inactivity.

(2) SELF-JUSTIFICATION

The words 'I', 'me' or 'my' occur nine times in the Hebrew in verses 2-3 alone. Jonah is totally wrapped up in his feelings. The simmering resentment he feels towards God bursts out in self-justifying poison. Just listen to him: 'O Lord, is this not what I said when I was still at home? That is why I was so quick to flee to Tarshish. I knew that you are a gracious and compassionate God, slow to anger and abounding in love, a God who relents from sending calamity.'

Jonah appeared to have made such strides after his experience of the storm and the whale, but indulging misguided thoughts have brought the return of all his old emotions and he is walking backwards. Jonah genuinely felt that God's readiness to forgive proved that his own initial instincts to opt out of this particular mission in the first place had been right all along. The Lord, he told himself, had been far too compassionate. The Ninevites had persuaded him to relent far too easily. Jonah may have repented from his earlier behaviour, but, on reflection, he was coming round to thinking that events had vindicated him. Jonah had been consistent throughout—it was God who had changed his mind.

(3) ACCUSATIONS

The flipside to self-justification is condemnation of others. 'If I am right,' one reasons, 'then the other person must be wrong.' In this case, Jonah believes he is right—so God must be in the wrong. As far as Jonah was concerned, the problem was not simply that the Lord was gracious and compassionate, slow to anger and abounding in love; it was more that he was *always* gracious and compassionate, slow to anger and abounding in love. His accusation was that the Lord should be able to discern those times when it was appropriate to be compassionate (and no doubt he could cite the example when he himself was in trouble in the fish) but there are other times when God ought to show a more ruthless streak. Clearly Jonah felt Nineveh was the classic example where their sin cried out for a firmer line—hence his anger against the Lord. Whatever happened to Jonah's promised song of thanksgiving (2:9)?

(4) IRRATIONALITY

Jonah's statement that he wanted to die (v. 4) is an attempt to impress God with just how strongly he feels about this matter. He has been here before (1:12). It sounds as though he has hit the rock-bottom of despair but, in truth, it is more a question of being irrational. A short while ago he had been offering a sacrifice of praise at having been delivered from drowning and from the belly of the whale. Now he wants to die. And what has intervened to make him change his mind? It was nothing other than a city-wide repentance, met by the grace of God. Jonah has allowed his feelings to dominate his thinking. No wonder he becomes irrational.

(5) FOLLY

In verse 5, Jonah builds himself a shelter, presumably from bits and pieces of dry branches lying around in the arid environment. It was probably a somewhat pathetic and rickety affair. There he sits, partly to sulk and partly to blackmail the Lord, telling himself and God that he will not budge until the Lord relents and destroys the Ninevites as promised. It is a sinfully dangerous game that he is getting into.

(6) LACK OF PERSPECTIVE

This point will only become clear in later verses, but the Lord is about to teach Jonah a valuable object lesson through a plant. As Jonah sits in sullen isolation, the Lord miraculously provides a vine that shoots up overnight. He awakens to find that his home-made shack has had a divine makeover. Structurally it has been made secure as the tendrils of the covering plant have bound it together; aesthetically it has been turned into a delightfully cool arbour by the luxuriant leaves.

In kindness, the Lord has provided the vine to give protecting shade for Jonah (v. 6), but Jonah's delight is wildly out of proportion. Because he has allowed his feelings to dictate his life, he has lost all sense of perspective. Euphoric over a plant and indifferent to the destruction of a city, he stands in need of divine instruction.

> There he sits, partly to sulk and partly to blackmail the Lord, telling himself and God that he will not budge until the Lord relents and destroys the Ninevites as promised. It is a sinfully dangerous game that he is getting into.

The Lord's question

In the midst of this, the Lord asks Jonah: 'Are you right to feel this way?' (v. 4) We as readers would look on and say, 'Of course he's not right.' Even Jonah himself does not seem overly confident in his position and declines to give an answer.

It is an important question because it shows us that the Lord expects an answer. In our culture we tend to the view that moods of whatever complexion are just 'one of those things'. Partly by temperament and partly by circumstances we excuse ourselves that they just come and there is not much that any of us can do about it. We would therefore dismiss the question as missing the point. However, the fact that the Lord asks it shows that we are responsible and answerable for our moods. We shall see next time that the Lord is not going to let Jonah get away with not answering the question. He will ask it again until he gets an answer.

FOR FURTHER STUDY

1. Read Jeremiah 12:1; 15:18 and 20:7 and consider how forthright the prophet was in pouring out the concerns of his heart to the Lord.

2. Read Exodus 34:6-7. Jonah's comments about the Lord's compassion are based on this passage.

3. Read Luke 15:1-2. Compare how Jonah takes an aspect of God's grace and kindness and turns it into a criticism of him with the way in which the Pharisees criticize Jesus for eating with sinners.

4. Read Isaiah 40:27-31. This is the antidote to the foolish thoughts expressed by the nation of Israel in the grip of a collective mood of self-pitying depression. The need is for them to be reminded of the solid realities of a compassionate, powerful God. They must wait for him and renew their strength like that of the eagles.

TO THINK ABOUT AND DISCUSS

1. The Lord has given us a mind which in Christ is renewed. If we are not to be ruled by our emotions, what place does passion and feeling have in the Christian life?

2. In what way is the shelter that Jonah built reminiscent of the vain attempts of mankind to save itself? Are there any parallels between the covering which the Lord provided for Jonah and the clothing he provided for Adam and Eve in Genesis 3?

3. We can always blame others for the way we are and the way we feel. We can even blame God indirectly for giving us the temperament we possess. Or we can blame something else—circumstances, tiredness, our hormones, etc. These help explain things, but if the Lord asks us to own our moods and answer for them, what does that mean in practice?

10 Sun, wind and worm

(4:7-11)

Once again Jonah and the Lord are locked in battle. It is not a fight between enemies but a struggle for mastery between friends. As a contest it is unequal and there will only ever be one victor, but the Lord's purpose in engaging in battle is not to punish Jonah. He wishes instead to teach him. Jonah will emerge from this conflict humbled and, we trust, more effective.

It is often the case that, in battles like this, the Lord uses an agent. In chapter one, for instance, he used a storm and a whale. In this chapter he again makes use of weather and animal together, but comes up with a different combination. This time it is sun, wind and worm. Just as the Lord had provided the great fish in 1:17 here, having provided a vine (v. 6), he now provides the worm (v. 7). The choice of food of a mighty fish is directed by the Lord, but so too is that of a little worm. A scorching east wind will shortly be provided also (v. 8).

The experience of battle in this final episode of the book exposes Jonah and reveals him in his true colours.

Jonah's heart revealed (v. 7)

In verse 6, we have seen Jonah deliriously, almost embarrassingly, happy. It is the happiest he has been, despite having been God's instrument for the most glorious spiritual revival the world has probably ever seen. His delight has been fuelled by the miraculous provision of a plant. Now he can sit in the cool of the shade and watch as Nineveh is destroyed. He knows that the vine is a divine gift, and it is possible that he sees it as the Lord's reconsideration of his decision to forgive Nineveh in the light of Jonah's personal protest. Jonah dares to believe that the Lord has come round to his way of thinking after all. If so, he takes it that the kind provision of a shade from the burning heat must be God's way of apologizing to him. This is vindication of the highest order.

With these delightful thoughts swimming around his head he sits down for a front-row viewing of the coming spectacle. But—and it is a big but—a tiny, insignificant worm is on its way. The worm is an ever-present reality in the context of death and decay (Mark 9:48). It is fitting that such a symbolic creature should be directed to be the means of highlighting the internal rottenness of Jonah's ethical code. On this occasion the early worm is on its way. As Rosemary Nixon points out, there is no early bird to stop it.

Jonah's temporary home has become his joy but it is about to be destroyed. Matthew Henry has these striking words:

See what all our creature-comforts are, and what we may

expect them to be; they are gourds, have their root in the earth, are but a thin and slender defence compared with the rock of ages; they are withering things, they perish in the using, we are soon deprived of them.

It was an act of compassion for the Lord to provide the covering protection for Jonah, but when his heart went after it, it was an even greater act of kindness for the Lord to remove it. In kindness the Lord may allow us our toys, but he can remove them at a stroke to teach us that our joy should be in him alone.

Jonah's folly revealed (v. 8)

As the new day dawns in verse 7, Jonah is completely oblivious to what awaits him. His anger has gone and there is much in life to delight him. Perhaps his spirits soar even higher as he senses the wind picking up and wonders if this is a harbinger of the storm of destruction about to engulf Nineveh.

But then the joy drains from him as he notices the leaves turning dry and brown before his very eyes. Maybe he inspects the base of the vine and realizes that it has been attacked. Perhaps he sees the worm and even stamps on it in frustrated anger. If so, it is too late. His beloved plant is gripped by death and he knows there is nothing he can do about it.

As the vine shrivels and dies, so the protecting and binding canopy over Jonah's little shelter drops away. At the mercy of the increasing wind the structure quickly disintegrates. Swept by swirling sand, the remnants of what was once his delightful abode are soon covered and lost to view. This is not a cool breeze but the hot sirocco wind that intensifies the heat. Jonah is left exposed in the searing temperatures. Just as the worm has attacked the plant, so now the sun gets up and attacks Jonah. He grows faint as the sun blazes down on his head (v. 8). It is probably a case of severe sunstroke. The full horror is beginning to dawn on him. This sand storm is not for Nineveh at all—it is for him!

> In kindness the Lord may allow us our toys, but he can remove them at a stroke to teach us that our joy should be in him alone.

At this point Jonah's folly is revealed. He knows that the vine is dead but wishes to go with it. Again, Matthew Henry sums it up well: 'Foolish man, that thinks his life bound up in the life of a weed.' In the first storm in chapter 1, Jonah had been brought to the edge of eternity, asking to be thrown overboard in preference to seeking the face of the Lord. Here in a second storm, he once again seeks the relief of death itself. The heat and the wind may have been unbearably fierce, but Jonah's readiness to opt out of life is becoming a habit. And it is all because he is not happy about God's mercy.

Jonah's emotions revealed (v. 9)

The death of the plant has re-kindled Jonah's anger. His joy lasted a day—equivalent to the life of his choice weed. But the appetite of a single worm has killed the plant and killed Jonah's happiness. His fury returns, having gone full circle. Last time round it was anger against God for the way in which he exercised his right to show mercy. This time it is

> The Lord asks Jonah to compare the vine with the city of Nineveh. That means a single, unfeeling plant against 120,000 morally illiterate people (although they were blameworthy in their wickedness, they were nevertheless spiritually ignorant).

anger against God for the way in which he exercises his right to destroy. Jonah believes passionately that the Lord has got things the wrong way round. Towards the Ninevites he should have shown the firm hand of justice—after all they deserved it. The plant, on the other hand, had only done good in its brief life. There was therefore every reason for the Lord to preserve its life.

Jonah's own suffering merely heightened the sense of unfairness that he felt towards God. In the background may have been unanswered questions as to why he had to face such repeated and severe ordeals for what he felt were fairly minor offences, when the violence and immorality of the Ninevites was met with nothing less than an absolute discharge and the full blessing of the judge. The thought that the Lord was playing with him was further provocation—why provide a vine for his comfort, only to take it away again? Nobody likes being mocked.

So when the Lord repeats the question of verse 4 and asks him whether he has a right to be angry, you can almost hear him spit the words out: 'I do. I am angry enough to die.'

Jonah's thinking exposed (vv. 10, 11)

Quiet reason does not always work when someone is in a foul mood. It is quite likely that it did not work here either—at least not immediately. Nonetheless it does not stop the Lord putting forward solid arguments as to why Jonah needs to think again. Having asked Jonah about his anger, the Lord will see the conversation through, wherever it leads. He could have rebuked Jonah for his discourteous reply or ignored him altogether, but once again the Lord chooses to answer the substance of Jonah's complaint.

> Jonah's emotions have all been directed at the life of the plant. God's passion has been directed at the life of Nineveh.

The Lord asks Jonah to compare the vine with the city of Nineveh. That means a single, unfeeling plant against 120,000 morally illiterate people (although they were blameworthy in their wickedness, they were nevertheless spiritually ignorant). Jonah had done nothing for the vine, whereas the Lord was behind both the plant and the city, in his role as creator and upholder of life. The vine shot up overnight, but the origins of Nineveh go back to the book of Genesis. The death of a plant may be one thing, but the destruction of human and animal life is another thing entirely.

Now, here is the point: both the Lord and Jonah have shown a tearful pity (as the word translated 'concerned' in verses 10 and 11 means in the original Hebrew). Jonah's emotions have all been directed at the life of the plant. God's passion has been directed at the life of Nineveh. The Lord does not tell Jonah that he is wrong to feel pity for the plant. Instead, he asks the simple question: 'Jonah, if you feel pity for the plant, why should I not be allowed to feel pity for the city?'

The unanswered question

The Lord has the last word in the book of Jonah, but since it is a question, the final word ought to belong to Jonah. Unlike his hasty response in verse 9, on this occasion there is no answer. There may be two reasons for the silence. First, the book is its own answer. In other words, the very fact that Jonah recorded his experience in self-effacing detail is as clear an indication as anyone could want that he understood the lessons the Lord had been teaching him. More than that, he absorbed those lessons and was anxious that others should also profit from reading the account. Had he walked away at the end of chapter 4, nursing his bitterness, there would have been no book of Jonah. Jonah's response, unrecorded as it is, can only be a full-hearted 'yes'.

The other reason for the silence is that if Jonah had recorded the answer he gave we would have missed the point that, in a sense, the question is directed at us. All of us who read the book of Jonah are required to give our own response. In our case, the thing we cherish is likely to be something other than a plant, but the point is still just as valid. How does the worth of an immortal soul stack up against our chosen toy, whatever that toy may be? The question is asked in terms of the souls of others, but it can also be asked of the individual's own soul. Jesus asked the same question in a slightly different form: 'What good will it be for a man if he gains the whole world, yet forfeits his soul? Or what can a man give in exchange for his soul?' (Matt. 16:26).

It is a question that is never answered just once, but needs constantly repeating. And it is the question with which the book fittingly closes.

For further study ▶

FOR FURTHER STUDY

1. See Luke 19:41-44. The Lord Jesus approached Jerusalem, saw it and wept over it. There were unique factors at work here: it was his own capital city, he foresaw its coming destruction, and it had had such a privileged past. Nonetheless, there are parallels with any other city or town in the world, past or present. The Lord is moved with pity when, whichever place it is, it hardens its heart against him and spurns the very things that would bring peace.

2. Read Hebrews 12:1-11. How should we look upon hardship? Why does God discipline his children?

TO THINK ABOUT AND DISCUSS

1. The Lord has laboured over Nineveh and laboured over Jonah himself. What is his purpose in these activities, and what does it tell us about his character?

2. We are warned not to make our treasures on earth (Matt. 6:19-21). Why not? What does it mean to store up treasures in heaven?

Additional Resources

Rosemary Nixon, *The Message of Jonah*, Bible Speaks Today Series, Inter-Varsity Press

T Desmond Alexander, *Jonah An Introduction and Commentary*, Tyndale Old Testament Commentaries, Inter-Varsity Press

John L Mackay, *Focus on the Bible—Jonah, Micah, Nahum, Habakkuk and Zephaniah*, Christian Focus Publications

Geoffrey T Bull, *The City and the Sign—an Interpretation of the Book of Jonah*, Hodder and Stoughton Ltd

Matthew Henry *A Commentary on the Holy Bible*

O Palmer Robertson, *Jonah—A Study in Compassion*, Banner of Truth

James Montgomery Boice *The Minor Prophets: Hosea—Jonah*, Baker Books

C F Keil Commentary on the Old Testament, *Vol X—Minor Prophets*, William B Eerdmans Publishing Company

Peter Williams, *Jonah: Running from God—An expositional commentary*, Day One Publications